Exhibit!

How to use exhibitions to grow your business

FIONA HUMBERSTONE

For Pete, Ellie and Jasper, with love

CONTENTS

PART ONE: ABOUT EXHIBITIONS

PART TWO: BEFORE THE EXHIBITION

PART THREE: AT THE EXHIBITION

PART FOUR: AFTER THE EXHIBITION

CASE STUDIES AND RECOMMENDED APPROACHES.

APPENDICES

FOREWORD

When I first wrote this book in 2009, Britain was mid recession and companies of all sizes were going under at an alarming rate.

We all needed to find cost effective ways of promoting our businesses and on the back of a set of marketing workshops I'd been running, I decided I'd put together a series of books that would provide small business owners with practical and cost effective ways of winning more business.

I had always found exhibitions to be a highly powerful way of building my business and wrote *Exhibit!* primarily as a resource for my customers.

This book is designed to inspire you to think differently about your next event. To plan your strategy, to gain in focus and to create simple yet powerful marketing

Use it as a guide, a toolkit to help you navigate your way through your next exhibition. Whether it's your first or your fifteenth, I hope that you gain something that you can put in place to boost your profits.

I sold my company in 2012 but the demand for a simple and practical guide to exhibiting continues. The recession may be (hopefully) coming to an end but the principles behind this book are just as relevant in good times as they are in times of economic crisis.

This second edition has undergone a very light edit: mostly just updating links and references and I've made a deliberate decision to leave my voice as it was when I wrote the book. You'll find references to what I do in my business in the present tense which I hope you'll find more inspiring and relevant to your situation.

I wish you lots of luck with your next exhibition.

Fiona Humberstone
May 2014
www.fionahumberstone.com

INTRODUCTION

So you've got an exhibition booked, or perhaps you're thinking of attending one. But you're nervous. You've heard horror stories of exhibitions swallowing up vast sums of cash for very little return. How do you make sure that your hard-earned cash doesn't go to waste?

Relax! This book will demonstrate how you can use exhibitions to build brand awareness, gain new clients and grow your profit. And the good news is that most of the tips I'm going to share with you are incredibly straightforward, and often, commonsense.

Exhibitions enable you to get out there and meet with your potential clients face-to-face, build relationships with them and put your company 'front of mind'.

I want to share with you the secrets behind one of the most powerful marketing activities my business does. I'll show you how to maximise your brand exposure, gain hundreds of quality leads and convert a high percentage of those into paying customers. I'll show you how to maximise the return on your investment in exhibitions, and I'll give you a process that will seriously boost your business.

Yet despite that, companies both large and small fail to capitalise on the potential of exhibitions because they don't manage the opportunity properly. They expect to turn up on the day, throw up a banner and gain thousands of pounds worth of business. And then they blame the organiser when it doesn't work.

This book will show you more than how to create an attractive exhibition stand. I'll show you how to plan, set goals and get ahead with your marketing literature so that you gain a significant return on your investment.

HOW I USE EXHIBITIONS TO ADD HUNDREDS OF NEW CLIENTS TO MY BUSINESS EVERY YEAR.

When I started my graphic design and print business in June 2005 I faced a challenge many start-ups face: great product, no clients and a chunky mortgage to pay. A truly terrifying combination!

Although I'd worked in the industry for several years, I hadn't been client facing for some time, so I brought no contacts with me and had no real potential for gaining any customers quickly.

I was operating from a serviced office in the centre of Guildford that, whilst central, was pretty invisible. So the chances of gaining passing trade were zero.

I needed to find a way of building up my business, and fast!

On my second day as my own boss, I exhibited at a local business-to-business event. By the end of the day I had captured around 100 leads. Over the following days, weeks and months I called, emailed and wrote to these leads, and within a year had converted almost 70% of those into paying customers.

Those 70 new customers told their friends about my business, who told their friends, and soon we had more work than we knew what to do with. Despite working just four days a week, I became one of the fastest growing start-up printing.com franchises.

I put that success down to a combination of gaining a large number of leads in just one day, and delivering a fantastic product and service.

I still believe that if I hadn't exhibited at that June exhibition, my business would not have taken off as rapidly as it did.

Sure, the business growth would not have happened if we hadn't had an attractive product at a price that people were prepared to pay. If we hadn't delivered exceptional service and great design I doubt that we would have been recommended. But five years on, I cannot think of a more cost-effective way of gaining a large number of quality leads that quickly.

As my business has grown, I have attended many more exhibitions. And over the years I've developed a process that has enabled me to make exhibitions one of the most profitable tools of my marketing strategy.

It's a process that enables me to maximise my brand exposure, gain high numbers of quality leads, and convert a high percentage of these into paying customers. And now I'm going to show you how it can do the same for your business.

THIS BOOK IS FOR YOU

This book is for the entrepreneurs, the small business owners, the kitchen table startups and the designer makers. It's for those of you following your passion, your dreams and really making a difference. It's for those of you with big ambitions who like most of us are being pulled in many directions.

You'll find plenty of inspiration, practical tips and thought provoking exercises to make sure that every penny you invest in an exhibition brings you a return.

I want to show you that **success** at an exhibition isn't a black art or the reserve of those with limitless budgets. Together we'll help you **focus** on what it is you really want to achieve from your next event and inspire you to create an impressive and **impactful** stand.

You'll discover some simple tips and tricks for creating **powerful** posters and marketing literature for the event and gain plenty of **insights** into what you need to do to make your next exhibition even more successful.

And if that meant helping you to do just one thing, I'd like to help you **win more profitable clients from your next exhibition**

THIS BOOK WILL HELP YOU:

1. Work out what's motivating visitors so that you can sell to them more effectively

2. Read a floorplan so that you can design the layout of your stand to create maximum impact

3. Gain an insight into how you can attract more visitors to your stand

4. Discover how to create a positive impression of your business without spending a fortune

5. Find a formula for creating posters with punch

6. Show you the twelve mistakes most businesses make when they attend an exhibition, and how you can avoid making the same mistakes

7. Save you from wasting time, money and effort when it comes to choosing your next show

8. Show you specific techniques for gaining quality leads and converting them into paying customers

9. Discover how to attract the right sort of customers who are prepared to spend what you want to charge

Getting more out of your next exhibition is what this book is all about. It's time to stop turning up to exhibitions just because your competitors are there. **It's time to start getting a real return on your investment.**

PART ONE: ABOUT EXHIBITIONS

WHY EXHIBIT?

I'm a huge fan of exhibitions because they've been so instrumental in the success of my own business. Over 30% of my clients have come from exhibitions and we have directly generated several hundred thousand pounds worth of revenue from these clients.

What I can't measure is the business that's been referred to us as a result of these clients recommending us to their friends. Realistically, that figure is likely to be significantly more but it's fair to say that exhibitions are an important part of my marketing strategy.

SOME OF THE BENEFITS OF EXHIBITING.

- You get to meet your customers face to face
- Networking with other businesses: both exhibitors and visitors
- Gaining leads
- Building your database
- Selling your products
- You can hear first hand 'the word on the street'
- Using the visitors to undertake market research
- Boosting your brand awareness
- You can launch a new product or service
- Recruitment of new franchisees, staff or distributors
- You can use it to educate your target audience
- It will support your other marketing efforts

Exhibiting also brings with it certain unique benefits that you simply would not gain from many other forms of marketing.

EXHIBITIONS BRING A TARGETED GROUP OF INDIVIDUALS TOGETHER

An exhibition like the Chelsea Flower Show brings together a group of people who are actively interested in gardening. These visitors have so much more than a passing interest because they have actually got out of their armchairs and come to Chelsea. That shows dedication and passion! What other forms of communication bring you that level of commitment?

EXHIBITIONS BRING YOUR POTENTIAL CUSTOMERS TO YOU

There's something very powerful about a visitor walking onto your stand or into your space. If cold calling or direct mail is all about you 'pushing' your services, exhibitions enable you to 'pull' in clients on their terms. OK, so they might just be interested in the free wine or doughnuts you have on offer, but we'll talk about how to get that working in your favour later in the book.

EXHIBITIONS ARE PERSONAL. THEY ENABLE YOUR COMPANY TO SHOW ITS' HUMAN FACE

Let's face it: people buy people. We like to buy from people we like, and people we have a relationship with. Here's your chance to bring your company to life and build relationships with the visitors to the show. And I'm not just talking about new leads. Take the opportunity to cement a relationship with your current customers: make them feel special, loved and important. Make a fuss of them and let potential customers see how well you treat your clients.

EXHIBITIONS BRING OUT THE 'SOUVENIR MENTALITY' IN PEOPLE

The vast majority of visitors coming to an exhibition want to take something home with them. Now that might be a plant from the Gardeners World Live event, a saucepan from the Ideal Home show or a pair of knickers from the National Wedding Show. It might be a business book or just a free goody bag. Whatever it is, you can take advantage of that mentality to sell your products.

EXHIBITIONS CREATE A LEVEL PLAYING FIELD

The fact is that people will make assumptions about how successful your business is based on how your exhibition stand looks and how your staff behave. The bad news is that if you're a successful company but you have a shabby stand people will be unimpressed. The good news is that even the smallest, micro business start-up can create a big impression with a bit of creativity and planning. The right first impression will seriously elevate your status and build reassurance.

WHY PEOPLE ATTEND EXHIBITIONS

Every year millions of people leave the comfort of their homes or offices and trek sometimes hundreds of miles to an exhibition or tradeshow. But why? Here are the main reasons.

TO GAIN IDEAS AND INSPIRATION

Most exhibitions pull in hundreds, if not hundreds of thousands, of visitors because of the promise of ideas and inspiration. 30% of visitors come to trade fairs specifically to look for new ideas and a staggering 73% to support their purchase decisions.

Think of the marketing exhibition that offers a day full of seminars on different ways you can market your business. Or the Good Food Show with live cookery demonstrations from celebrity chefs.

Ideas and inspiration are likely to be what the bulk of visitors are looking for: how can you give ideas and inspiration to this group of people?

TO MEET NEW SUPPLIERS OR STRATEGIC PARTNERS

People new to an industry will often be interested in meeting new suppliers. I can remember attending the Direct Marketing show almost a decade ago now simply because I wanted to see what was out there.

These visitors are likely to methodically walk around every stand to make sure they don't miss anything! They'll also scour the exhibition guide if they're short on time and cherry-pick the suppliers they most want to meet.

Be sure that your showguide and website entry is enticing enough to attract as many visitors as possible. We cover this in Chapter Three.

TO NETWORK

Many visitors will want to network: with the exhibitors, with other visitors and with the expert speakers. This is much more true of business-to-business events, but even if you're at a consumer show make sure you connect with other exhibitors.

Even if you can't see how the person on your stand will directly benefit your business, it's good to connect. You never know who they might know or who they may be able to introduce you to, so take the time to chat, build relationships and see which of your contacts you can introduce them to on the day – they'll thank you for it!

TO BE SEEN

Especially true of industry-specific and local business exhibitions. Many visitors will want to come simply to build their profile and show the key players that they're still around!

FOR THE FREEBIES

Exhibitions do strange things to even the most reserved Brit. Any chance of a freebie and we're on a mission to get ours before they go – I call them Freebie Hunters. You see them at farmer's markets, grazing on the free tastings at every stall - haven't we all done it? And you see them at business exhibitions too – grabbing every carrier bag, pen, ruler and sweetie in sight!

It's easy to be disparaging towards the Freebie Hunters but why not use this condition in your favour? Create exciting-looking, branded goody bags and you'll bring those Freebie Hunters to your stand, plus gain a lot of extra brand exposure.

BECAUSE THEY HAVE NOTHING BETTER TO DO!

Yes, honestly. There are a group of people (also known as Tyrekickers) who will amble around an exhibition, spending hours chatting to you simply because they have nothing better to do. If you like a challenge, and you're not rushed off your feet, these people are still worth connecting with – even if they are not looking for themselves, they might have friends who need you.

TO LEARN ABOUT A NEW SUBJECT

People that are new to an industry will often visit an exhibition to see what's out there. This is particularly true of something like a wedding show where most brides, before they get engaged, have absolutely no idea of this industry. A well-designed stand with presence, and helpful, charming stand staff are essential to showing these visitors that you mean business.

TO CHECK OUT THE COMPETITION

So these visitors decided not to exhibit this year, but they thought they'd come along and see what everyone else does so that they can do it better next year. Show them you mean business with a fantastic stand and great take-home material.

TO MAINTAIN CONTACT WITH SUPPLIERS OR CLIENTS

One of the real benefits local exhibitions and industry tradeshows offer the visitors is saving time. Rather than travelling around the country setting up individual meetings, the show enables people to meet with suppliers and clients in one place.

It's highly likely that there will be visitors from all of these camps at your exhibition and successful exhibiting is about understanding why visitors are coming to the event so that you can match their expectations. We'll come back to that later in the book.

HOW TO USE EXHIBITIONS TO GROW YOUR BUSINESS

Are you someone who starts thinking about your exhibition a week or two before the event? Perhaps you wake up the day before the show thinking **"Yikes! We've got an exhibition tomorrow!**" And so you madly dash around trying to pull together posters and a leaflet to make your stand look half decent.

I'm someone who thrives on last minute decisions, high pressure and tight deadlines, but I've come to realise that when it comes to exhibitions, the more prepared I can be, the better. There are really three key stages to a successful exhibition, and I've tried to reflect these in this book.

Firstly some careful planning to make sure you create a real splash at the show and are fully equipped with the right marketing materials. I find it really helps to get ahead by writing sales letters and email follow-ups in advance, as well as blocking out a couple of days to start on the follow-up.

The big day itself: a whirlwind of people, hot leads and of course those slightly annoying people that try to sell their services to you on your stand, you'll find them at every show.

Finally the aftermath, when it's so easy to get sucked back in to your day job that maximising the potential of your new contacts goes by the wayside. We'll look at how you take that shoebox full of leads and turn them into profitable clients.

Throughout the book you'll find action points and exercises designed to help you really absorb what I'm sharing with you. You'll find this especially useful if you have a specific exhibition in mind. I've also included plenty of examples, case studies, suggestions and documents to help you really maximise the potential of your next event.

THE KEY TO EXHIBITING SUCCESSFULLY.

- Pick the right exhibition
- Set SMART goals
- Create a stand with wow factor
- Have some powerful marketing literature
- Run a can't-miss-it competition to capture data
- Follow up quickly, comprehensively and persistently

This, in a nutshell, is what you need to do if you want to make your next exhibition a profitable part of your marketing activity. You see? It's probably not groundbreaking, but so many businesses fail to do any or all of this process, and that's why exhibitions don't work for them.

FOUR THINGS TO KNOW ABOUT GAINING PROFITABLE CLIENTS FROM EXHIBITIONS

1. UNDERSTAND WHY PEOPLE ARE HERE

If you were to stand on the exits at your next exhibition and ask 50 or 100 people what had motivated them to clear their day and attend, I guarantee that the vast majority of them would not say that the sole reason was wanting to see your business. The range of businesses at exhibitions is a pull for many people, but you must realise that most visitors won't be making a beeline for your stand: there are lots of other distractions and you need to persuade them that it's a good idea to come and chat to you. That's harder than it sounds, but I'll give you plenty of tips and inspiration to make this a doddle.

2. RUN AN IRRESISTIBLE, AND RELEVANT, COMPETITION TO CAPTURE DATA

The sad fact is that even if you made a great first impression on the day, by the time your visitors get on the train home they will have forgotten about the vast majority of exhibitors. How you communicate with these visitors afterwards is the key to how much business you win from your next show. And the best way to be able to communicate with visitors is to run an irresistible, and relevant, competition to capture your visitors contact details.

3. KEEP IN TOUCH WITH PEOPLE REGULARLY AFTER THE EVENT

Even if you're selling products at an exhibition, the sales you make on the day are just the tip of the iceberg. The real value in exhibitions is being able to build up a targeted mailing list - as long as you make sure you use it, that is.

4. CREATE A STAND THAT DOES YOUR BUSINESS JUSTICE

Visitors will form an impression, positive or negative, based on how your company appears at this exhibition. Make sure you create a positive impression.

"BUT EXHIBITIONS DON'T WORK FOR MY BUSINESS"

Perhaps they don't. However my hunch is that it's not that exhibitions don't work per se, but more likely that you haven't managed the opportunity effectively enough.

Generating a profit from an exhibition isn't easy. It will take you time and money, but boy is it worth it! **Quite simply, my business would not be where it is today if it weren't for exhibitions.** I've generated several hundred thousand pounds worth of revenue from the clients I've gained from exhibitions. Let's work through my process so that you can do the same.

We've already established that far from there being a 'secret code' you need to crack to have success at exhibitions, you just need to use your common sense. And that starts with understanding a bit more about exhibitions, what they're good for, what they're bad for and why so many businesses fail to win profitable clients from them.

Let's start by looking at how exhibitions can benefit your business.

WHAT EXHIBITIONS ARE GOOD FOR

Exhibitions are **great for building your database**, making new contacts, showing the human side of your company and building your profile. As we discussed earlier, exhibitions bring a very targeted group of interested individuals together in one place. If you can capture their contact details you can build a relationship over time and gain lots of profitable clients. The secret is to make sure you're at the right exhibition in the first place and that you have plenty of marketing activity planned to build a meaningful relationship with your self selected contacts after the show.

EXHIBIT! HOW TO USE EXHIBITIONS TO GROW YOUR BUSINESS

Exhibitions are **great for start-up businesses and micro businesses** because you have the opportunity to compete with the more established, larger players. At an event, visitors aren't judging you on the size of your office or how fancy your reception desk looks, they're looking at your stand – which will work for or against you depending on how fabulous your stand looks.

There's still a place in your marketing mix for exhibitions if you run a more established company too. It's likely that your database will still benefit from an influx of highly targeted people, and you'll also be able to use the event to **boost the awareness of your brand**. I've learned that marketing is quite a lot like gardening: if you do a little bit every week, year on year you'll find it's really productive. Some of the real successes from exhibitions come from you being there year on year and establishing a real presence within your target market. Don't underestimate the power of brand awareness, it goes hand in hand with powerful marketing.

Exhibitions are also great platforms for **networking** with other exhibitors and building firm relationships with your existing clients. Take advantage of the hospitality facilities to buy your clients a drink and have a chat with them on 'neutral' territory. You'll find you build stronger relationships with them that way.

In fact, a friend of mine tells how one of his most successful exhibitions came about when he gave each of his staff a £500 subsistence budget and told them to set up meetings with their clients. Needless to say a good time was had by all and some great sales relationships forged from that day. I suspect that in todays leaner times that approach might not be so practical but the point is that building relationships with people, bonding and finding things in common with each other is never a bad thing.

WHAT EXHIBITIONS ARE BAD FOR

The real strength of exhibitions is in the sheer volume of targeted visitors they bring. So I would strongly advise you against using all your resources on a long, consultative sale. In most cases, exhibitions are the place where people will go to gather information, so it's unlikely that you'll close a big, complex sale. That's not to say it won't happen, but generally it's not the case.

For example, if I was selling earrings at £25 a pair I could rightly expect to close a lot of deals at an exhibition. If I went to the National Franchise Exhibition with my franchise that required an investment in excess of £100,000 it's highly unlikely that I'd close a deal at the show. What I would do is be able to gain a list of very hot leads that I'd be able to move further along the sales funnel, and another, much larger list of people interested in buying a franchise that I could build a relationship with after the event.

TYPES OF EXHIBITIONS

I've loosely used the word exhibition or show to cover a multitude of events where a group of organisations are gathering together to promote their products and services to visitors.

You might find yourself exhibiting at:

TRADE SHOWS Most industries will run a trade show on an annual basis. These shows bring together industry experts, suppliers and companies all in one place. The focus of these events is on networking, giving and sharing information and launching the latest products or services. The Mortgage Business Expo, Top Drawer and Multimodal, a freight industry exhibition, all bring together a very targeted group.

CONFERENCES combined with exhibitions are quite possibly my favourite type of events. I love the fact that the conference agenda pulls together a group of visitors who have one interest in common. Grow Your Business in Surrey is a great example of this type of event.

LOCAL BUSINESS-TO-BUSINESS EXHIBITIONS are often run by the local Chamber of Commerce or networking group as a showcase for local businesses. They're a useful way to raise your profile with people interested in doing business locally. Don't expect them to have the focus of a conference, as the net is usually cast far and wide which may sometimes mean that the visitors don't have as much relevance to your business as a conference might.

EDUCATIONAL EVENTS careers fairs, freshers' fairs, or 'what next' type of events. Although in this book I mostly talk about "selling" and "gaining clients" the principles apply just as well to not-for-profit organisations looking to recruit candidates or influence choices of education.

LARGE CONSUMER SHOWS such as the long running Ideal Home Show, and more recently Grand Designs Live, attract hundreds of thousands of visitors. Many of these visitors are attracted by the celebrity endorsement and are looking for a good day out as much as they're looking to gain information. One of the big benefits of these types of show is that like conferences, they bring together a very targeted group of people. Other events of this type include the Caravan and Motorhome Show, The Baby Show, the Luxury Travel Fair and Top Gear Live.

CRAFT FAIRS, FLOWER SHOWS AND AGRICULTURAL SHOWS attract a public looking for entertainment. At the CLA Game Fair, the RHS Flower Shows and the County Shows that spring up around the country the focus isn't on the exhibition, it's generally on the entertainment in the arenas: from sheep shearing to showjumping. However, the exhibition stands are a huge part of the event. Many visitors will go expecting to spend money, and the chances are that especially if you offer an incentive to buy, you'll sell a lot at these shows. That said, there's still a lot of potential for you to build your database, so don't overlook my guidance on capturing data: you'll be missing a big opportunity if you don't.

WHEN IT DOESN'T WORK

Why do most companies fail to generate a decent return from exhibitions?

Quite simply because they don't manage the opportunity effectively.
Ask your business network how they find exhibitions. You'll probably get some pretty mixed feedback. Any of these responses sound familiar? **"We don't find that exhibitions work for us."** or **"We attended an exhibition last year and to be honest it didn't pay off"**

The sad fact is that many businesses, large and small sink thousands, if not tens of thousands, of pounds in to exhibitions every year: and very few of them see a decent return.

Is this because exhibitions are expensive branding exercises? Is it because most exhibition organisers don't pull their weight when it comes to promotion? In the vast majority of cases I would say not. It's usually because the exhibitor has failed to make the most of the opportunity.

THE TOP TWELVE REASONS THAT COMPANIES FAIL TO MAKE A SUCCESS OF EXHIBITIONS.

Let's start by taking a look at what not to do, so that you can put strategies in place to get your next exhibition right.

1. THEY WERE AT THE WRONG EXHIBITION.

It's easy just to sign up to an exhibition because your competitors are there or you think it's a great opportunity.

Remember how I told you about the first exhibition I attended where I gained 100 leads and converted 70 of those into paying clients? Well I'm afraid I thought I'd cracked it! I thought that every exhibition would give me the same return.

And so when another exhibition came up four months later, I jumped at the chance to attend. I was disappointed to say the least at the 38 leads we gained, and even more so at the quality of the leads – we converted less than 25% into paying clients. And I learned a valuable lesson: to **look at the opportunity on offer before diving in with my chequebook**.

2. THEY DIDN'T MAKE THEIR OFFERING RELEVANT TO THE VISITORS

The vast majority of visitors haven't come to the exhibition to see your business. They probably don't even know who you are or what you do. Which means that there is absolutely no point in throwing up a generic poster or pop-up stand. You need to **refine your offering and make it relevant to the visitors at this specific exhibition**.

3. THEY DIDN'T CAPTURE ENOUGH LEADS

There are many reasons to exhibit and the main one for me is to use exhibitions to capture leads and build my database. I'll sell later, at the exhibition it's a frantic mission to capture as many leads as possible. And that's the way I like it! Forget to ask for a card, don't bother to record the data you've gathered and there's no surprise that exhibitions don't work. We cover strategies to help you generate the right sort of leads later in the book.

4. THEY DIDN'T FOLLOW UP THE LEADS

I recently worked one to one with a company helping them plan their exhibition strategy for a new product they were launching. We started talking about the owner's previous experience of exhibitions and I asked him how many leads they'd generated in the past. "Not many" was his response. And so I asked him how much business he'd generated from those leads "Erm… I'm not sure" came the reply "they're still in the shoebox from last year."

It's a rare exhibitor that doesn't make a token gesture to gain at least some leads. However so many exhibitors get home exhausted, with a shoebox full of leads. What do they do with them? They 'file' them away in the office, never to be looked at again. An absolutely heinous crime! No wonder they didn't win any business. Their competitors were too busy contacting all the show visitors and the potential clients went for the easy option: the company that kept in touch.

Plan ahead to make sure that your follow up is as effective as possible. We look at this in Chapter Five.

5. THEIR STAND LOOKED UNINSPIRING

I realise that given my background I'll be more picky than most about the way your stand looks, but you cannot underestimate the importance of making sure your stand looks fabulous.

What people often do is spend their entire exhibition budget on the stand itself, leaving nothing for dressing it or creating any literature.

Your stand is your shop window for the day. It's how your potential clients will judge you. If your stand looks like you've penny-pinched and thrown it together at the last minute, what does that say about how you're going to handle your customers? See Part Four for my top tips for creating an inspiring exhibition stand.

6. THEIR MARKETING LITERATURE LET THEM DOWN

I once visited an exhibition where a courier was sharing a stand with an electrician. The stand was a curious mix of day-glo A4 posters from the courier, and plugs and raw wires on the electricians' half. It was hard to see the link between the two businesses, and not only did the stand lack polish, the marketing literature this courier was handing out betrayed his professionalism and passion for customer service. Sadly he is no longer in business and I can't help wondering whether an opportunity like a successful exhibition would have turned his business around and brought him a much-needed influx of new business.

Your marketing literature is all people have to remember you by once they are home from the event. Make sure yours leaves a confident and positive impression. You'll find insights into creating the right marketing literature later on in the book.

7. THEY DIDN'T HAVE A CLEAR OBJECTIVE FOR THE EVENT

There's nothing wrong with exhibiting purely as a way to get your name out there, but it becomes a pretty expensive networking event if that's your approach. As a small business owner I need to make sure that every piece of marketing I do generates a return on my investment, and exhibitions are no different. I go in with a clear goal to generate a specific number of leads, and we always make sure we exceed them.

What I know is that the vast majority of businesses that claim exhibitions don't work find it's because they haven't planned sufficiently. Ask them what they hoped to get out of the event and you gain a vague "more business" response. If you want to get "more business" then you need to plan to take very specific steps in order to achieve this.

Last year I worked one to one with an IT company on their exhibition stand. We set a goal of picking up more than 100 leads for this particular event and the Marketing Manager offered a prize for the person who generated the most leads. Her team were clear about what was required for the day, and guess what? They achieved their goals and picked up over 140 leads.

8. THEY DIDN'T LOOK WELCOMING OR FRIENDLY

How many exhibitions have you been to where the stand staff are huddled together in a corner chatting? Or looking menacingly at you from behind a clipboard? Or eating? Or on the phone? I could go on, but you get the picture...

As a visitor exhibition stands can be intimidating places. Do we dare cross that threshold into the bright lights? Worse still if I have to step up, even just 10cm! Are the stand staff going to bully me into buying something I don't want? Will I have to make a commitment? You've got to be pretty keen on a company to cross their threshold and join them on the stand.

9. THEY DIDN'T HAVE ENOUGH TAKE-AWAY LITERATURE

I recently caught up with a client of ours who had just had a particularly successful exhibition. She runs a jewellery company and had arranged for a hairdresser to come to the stand to demonstrate how jewellery and hair could work well together. This was a fantastic approach that generated crowds of people and doubled their sales from her last event! There were so many customers on the stand that there was no way the stand team could talk to them all (note to get more helpers for next year!) and so clients were walking away.

Plenty of take-away literature reminding customers of any special show offers is absolutely essential if you want to maximise your exposure and the business on the day.

10. THEY DIDN'T PROMOTE THEIR ATTENDANCE AT THE EVENT

When an event doesn't quite go to plan it's all too easy to blame the organisers. They didn't promote the exhibition well enough or ask the right people or put on an enticing enough seminar programme. And this may be true to a certain extent. But as an exhibitor you need to get involved with marketing the event too. You need to let people know that you're going to be there, because for some visitors, your attendance alone will be a big pull!

What can you do to encourage more of your contacts to visit you at your next show?

11. THEY WEREN'T PERSISTENT ENOUGH IN THEIR FOLLOW UP

Following up on every single lead after an exhibition is hard work, believe me. When you have over 100 leads, making a commitment to speak to every single one takes weeks, if not months of dedication. Often you won't get through straight away, and when you do your contact won't have time to talk and you'll need to call them back another time. But you've got to do it if you want to maximise on the opportunity. It will pay off.

Of course it doesn't just have to be you – it could be a telemarketing company or another member of staff, but **if you really want to make the most out of your leads, someone from your company must talk to them**.

12. THEY DIDN'T FOLLOW UP FOR LONG ENOUGH

With most companies, the average buying cycle is more than a couple of days, which means that sending out one email and a letter after the event just isn't going to cut it when it comes to winning business from your new contacts. **Plan to keep in touch for more than a year** and you'll get a considerably more profitable outcome from your new contacts.

NOW LET'S LOOK AT HOW TO DO IT THE RIGHT WAY...

I've shared the how-not-to-do-it list. Now let's take a look at how you can maximise your brand exposure, gain scores of leads and win plenty of business. Prepare to plan for your most successful exhibition yet!

PART TWO: BEFORE THE EXHIBITION

PLANNING FOR SUCCESS

In this section we're going to look at the steps you need to take to go into your next event fully prepared. I'll show you how to choose the right exhibition, how to pick the right spot and how to design your stand. We'll think about the marketing collateral you're going to need and I'll give you plenty of insights into how to make this work for you. Finally we'll look at seminars and speaking, pre-show publicity plans and what literature and giveaways you need to think about.

Let's start by planning.

SETTING GOALS

Life is busy. We're all plagued by our ever-growing "to-do" lists and I think we've all suffered from the temptation to dash out a piece of marketing without putting the right amount of thought into it. The problem is, we rarely get the result we want.

Whether you're putting together a leaflet, email marketing campaign, website or exhibition stand, so often we'll look back on these events and be disappointed that they didn't work. Why? Usually the root cause of the problem is the same: a lack of objective.

I'm convinced that business owners who claim exhibitions don't work for them are the ones who didn't think about what they wanted out of the event until afterwards.

It's easy to set retrospective goals when you find you didn't get the result you wanted. But if you create some aims from the outset, well you might just achieve them!

Setting an objective means that several wonderful things happen. Firstly, by defining what you want to get out of any piece of marketing you've started on the first step to making that happen. Secondly you can put small steps in place to ensure that your goal happens. Thirdly, you have created a measurement mechanism so that a day, a month, a year down the line you can measure whether you've achieved your goals.

SMART goals are the first step to success.

WHAT ARE SMART GOALS?

SMART goals are:

- **S**pecific
- **M**easurable
- **A**chievable
- **R**ealistic
- **T**imed

Setting SMART goals will increase your chances of achieving them because they force you to think realistically about what's possible and how you make that happen. SMART goals also mean that you rely less on emotional judgements such as how you feel the day has gone and are able to look more analytically at how it's actually performed.

For example, many people would go to an exhibition hoping to pick up "some leads" or "some business". That's a tricky one to measure.

I'm always very focused at my events and my goals for the Grow Your Business event from 2009 were to:

- **Gain 100 leads on the day** (I can measure that, they're specific, I know I can achieve them and I've put in a timing mechanism – one day!)
- **Convert 60 of those into paying customers within a year** (I can measure this and I know it's realistic because I've done better than this in the past)

In actual fact we gained more than 190 leads and are well on the way to meeting our target of 60 clients, and that's just two months on. I'll share how I make sure I convert a high percentage of leads into paying clients later on in the book.

Let's start by thinking about some ideal goals, and then we can make them SMART.

SOME SMART GOALS

DO YOU WANT TO CAPTURE AS MANY LEADS AS POSSIBLE?

This is my method of choice. I use the show as a data mining exercise and worry about converting into clients later. If you go down this route, what's realistic? When I talk about 100 leads I'm thinking of shows with 500-1000 visitors. So I'm aiming to capture 10-20% of visitors. What do you feel would be a realistic figure based on your experience and target audience?

Bear in mind that this figure will vary depending on what you do and the type of show you are booked in for.

DO YOU WANT TO SELL A PRODUCT, SERVICE OR SUBSCRIPTION?

If so, how many? How much revenue would you like to generate? Think about how you'll make this work. Are people likely to make a decision at the show there and then? Or is it a high ticket item they'll need to think about? Can you do anything to encourage them to buy there and then? Perhaps a one-off show discount?

David Austin roses had an irresistible offer on at this year's Hampton Court Flower Show which meant that rather than simply researching my roses of choice I ended up walking away with no less than six specimens on the day.

DO YOU WANT TO TAKE BOOKINGS FOR AN EVENT?

When we created a stand for a property investment company at 'A Place In the Sun' their goal was to get people booking site trips to the investment properties in Bulgaria and the Algarve. We made sure that every part of the stand and show was geared up to achieving this outcome.

DO YOU PLAN TO DISTRIBUTE AS MUCH INFORMATION AS POSSIBLE?

Do you have a target number of leaflets/ information packs you'd like to get rid of? This is often very appropriate for not for profit organisations or charities: you may not be interested in selling or generating leads. Perhaps you simply wish to enthuse and inform visitors Think about setting up demonstrations, interactive events and handing out goody bags.

IF YOU'RE A RECRUITER DO YOU HAVE A SET NUMBER OF CANDIDATES YOU'D LIKE TO FIND?

You might be looking for potential franchisees, people for a specific role or a voluntary organisation. In this case you're probably not looking to sell in the conventional sense of the word, but you want to gain details of suitable candidates.

✎ Exercise: Creating SMART Goals.

What, specifically do you want to achieve?	
How can you quantify your goal? Is it measurable?	
Is it achievable? Do you need to draft in extra resources?	
Is your goal realistic? Can you root it in any previous experience?	
When would you like to have achieved your goal by?	

We recently worked with a web design company who created some very ambitious goals for one of their exhibitions. They hoped to pick up fifty leads (fairly realistic) and convert 50% of those into paying clients within three months. Three months on, goal achieved!

SETTING A REALISTIC BUDGET

Budgeting is not about spending as little money as possible. It's about working out a realistic amount of money to spend and then making sure you keep within those constraints.

The problem with the 'spend as little as possible' approach it is rarely realistic and may often result in a poor impression. Remember that first impressions count at an exhibition.

Your exhibition stand will either reinforce or undermine your brand, and so often the stands done 'on the cheap' utterly destroy a company's branding. Not the impression you want to be giving prospective clients. People want to be sure that they're spending their money with the right company, so you need to be sure you send out the right signals.

Exhibitions, like most forms of marketing, cost time and money. And exhibitions in particular can cost a lot of money. But if you plan properly, create a fabulous stand and follow up properly afterwards it will pay off.

My very first exhibition cost around £2000 by the time I factored in my stand, giveaways, posters and marketing collateral. That's not allowing for any opportunity cost of us being there or following up afterwards.

In hindsight that doesn't seem like an enormous amount of money, but for many business start-ups that's a frightening amount to spend in one go.

It all comes down to return on investment. I gained 100 leads from that event, at a cost of just £20 per lead. And by converting 70% of those into paying clients that's a cost of around £25 per customer, which is a very low sum of money.

✎ Exercise: Work out your event budget.

Item	£
Stand and shell scheme	
Accommodation if it's not local to you	
Travel: train or plane fares, petrol, parking	
Meals while you're away	
Water, sandwiches on the day of the event	
Posters	
Pop-up or pull-up stands	
Leaflets, flyers, postcards	
Brochures	
Promotional giveaways: mugs, memory sticks etc	
Sweets or chocolates for your stand	
Flowers	
Stand styling props	
Graphic design	
Furniture purchase/ hire	
Staff costs: your regular staff plus extras	
AV hire: lighting, plasma screens, sound system	
Product samples	
Electricity, Internet connections	
Copywriting and website costs	
Total Cost of Exhibition	£

Don't just pluck figures out of the air. Research the costs, write a proper budget and work out how many new customers you'll need for the exhibition to pay for itself.

 # Calculating the cost per client.

Average conversion rate x Number of leads

Total cost of exhibition

Perhaps this looks a little scary! But how much would your average client spend in a year? Better still, your average new client spend. Do you have those figures to hand? If so, marvellous! If not, see the section on Key Performance Indicators in the Follow Up section for how...

OVERWHELMED BY THE COST OF THIS EXHIBITION?

How can you trim the figures without impacting on your professionalism? Do you really need those dancing girls and the champagne bottle giveaways?

Bear in mind as well that every business needs to invest money in marketing. No one is suggesting that exhibitions are cheap, but planned and managed properly they are highly effective.

And don't get sucked into thinking that you can get away without spending a penny on marketing your business. You need to find a number of routes to market: email marketing and social networking is not enough on it's own.

Even social networking costs you money. OK, so you might not pay a subscription fee for Twitter or Facebook (yet) but my goodness do they take time to use effectively. Don't underestimate the value of your time. Time spent marketing is time you can't be producing paid work – so your 'free' marketing does have a cost implication too.

When you think about costs, **think about the lifetime value of each client** as well as their initial purchase. If your average client orders three times a year and spends £300 each time then each client is worth about £900 a year. How many years do your clients stay with you on average? If it's three years then each client is worth about £2,700 in their lifetime. Does that make the exhibition spend seem a little bit better?

 *Calculating the value per client.*

Average customer spend per year x Average number of years clients buy from you

CHOOSING THE RIGHT EXHIBITION

In the introduction, I shared with you my early exhibition successes. This journey hasn't been without its challenges, however I'm a firm believer that if things don't quite go to plan, then you take a step back and look at why, and you'll ensure that next time things work much, much better.

Buoyed up by the success of my very first June exhibition I immediately signed up for another exhibition a couple of months later. This event was quite a different story. Although the event was cheaper, the volume of visitors was much lower. I received significantly fewer leads and I converted even less of those into paying clients.

I learned a valuable lesson from this: look properly at how the event is being marketed before you sign up.

I realised that, looking back at the event publicity, the exhibition was really a showcase of local businesses. In stark contrast to "Winning Business", an event that was a perfect fit for my new business. Seminars were the main focus of the day, which gave successful, busy business owners a reason to leave their desks. By contrast, this second event offered visitors the opportunity to "come and see what local businesses have to offer".

In hindsight, the types of business owners who had time to simply walk around an exhibition to see what was on offer, were probably not my target audience. I'm not knocking what has become an incredibly successful event; many exhibitors come back year after year, but for my business, my goals, this was the wrong event.

When I became involved with the Surrey-based event Grow Your Business, I was determined that we would offer a full seminar programme that would attract successful, busy business owners looking for new ideas and inspiration. Why? Because those were my target clients! And I felt that many other exhibitors would benefit from this type of ambitious, successful client too.

So if all exhibitions are not created equal, how do you find the right event for your business? Let's take a look.

FIND AN EXHIBITION THAT WORKS FOR YOUR BUSINESS NEEDS

I firmly believe that companies that say exhibitions don't work for them are simply exhibiting at the wrong events, or not marketing themselves properly at the right events. Before you sign on the dotted line, think carefully about whether the event is going to be right for your business.

UNDERSTAND WHY YOU'RE EXHIBITING

If this hard work and investment is going to pay off, you've got to be clear about why you're exhibiting. What do you want to achieve? Are you looking to:

- Build brand awareness of your business?
- Gain leads?
- Sell your products or services?
- Test a new product?
- Undertake market research?
- Go because your competitors are there? (this is NOT a reason in itself! Although it might be the motivating factor to get you to sign on the dotted line, you will not get a return on your investment without goals – see Before the Exhibition)
- Something else?

What's your goal? Do you think this exhibition provides you with an opportunity to achieve this?

WHERE IS THE EVENT?

Are the prospects you pick up going to travel to you? Or is geography irrelevant? It might be if you're providing a nationwide or online service, for example.

As a printing.com franchise there's probably not much point in me exhibiting in London, as there are several other outlets there that most clients would probably use rather than trek out to Guildford. **How well does the location work for you?**

WHO ARE THE VISITORS GOING TO BE?

Think about your most profitable clients. You know, the ones who really value what you do. The ones who are prepared to pay what you want to charge. The ones you love to work with. What do they look like? Where do they hang out? What are their challenges? Are you likely to find them at this exhibition?

ARE THE PEOPLE COMING TO THIS EXHIBITION PART OF YOUR TARGET AUDIENCE?

You don't need to get formal and delve deeply into visitor demographics. Simply talk to the organisers – who do they think the visitors will be, why are they coming to the event? You can do quite a lot of educated guesswork by looking at the marketing materials too.

If it's a business-to-business show, look at target company size, number of employees, turnover. And if it's a consumer show look at the mix of male to female visitors, their socioeconomic group and see if the organisers can give you any insight into their buying habits. The point is that an exhibition is only going to be as good as its' visitors. If they're not right for your business, why waste your time?

You'll find an exercise at the end of this chapter to help you focus on your target audience.

WHY ARE THE VISITORS ATTENDING?

Look at the angle the exhibition organisers are taking. How relevant is this angle to the products and services your business provides?

If you run an architectural practice, a show like Grand Designs Live may be the perfect place to pick up new business: tens of thousands of visitors are coming to the show because they are particularly interested in design and home improvements. The trick then, is to make sure that you attract only those visitors who are interested in having an architect work for them.

HOW MANY VISITORS ARE EXPECTED TO ATTEND?

This won't necessarily make or break your success as it's about quality rather than quantity, but it's always useful to have as a guide, and to compare against past and future exhibitions. I usually expect to pick up at least 10% of visitors as leads, 20% if I'm speaking or it's a particularly good show. At recent shows I have gained more than 25% of visitors' business cards. I suspect this is because I have sponsored the last couple of shows we have done and I've also presented seminars which has boosted our profile.

When you're calculating how many leads you'd like to generate do bear in mind that exhibition organisers are often optimistic about visitor numbers!

HOW WELL IS THE EVENT BEING MARKETED?

What plans do the organisers have for marketing the event? Read the show website – do you think it will attract your target audience?

HOW MANY STANDS WILL THERE BE?

This is usually quite a good gauge as to how big the show will be, and perhaps how much investment you want to put in. I'm not suggesting that small shows are bad, but you might want to scale back your investment (and your expectations!).

ARE ANY OF YOUR COMPETITORS ATTENDING?

You're not a sheep, you don't need to follow your competitors slavishly. But, if you have a more compelling proposition for this audience than your competitors, I'd suggest that you'll want to be there.

HAS THE SHOW BEEN ENDORSED OR SPONSORED BY ANY IMPORTANT INDUSTRY FIGURES?

Celebrities, industry experts and professional bodies all make a difference to the success of a show. They'll bring in more visitors, make the show more credible and often attract more media attention.

Grand Designs Live is an excellent example of this. Kevin McCloud and chums pull a great crowd, and are the icing on the cake for a show packed with seminars, practical demonstrations and show homes. It might seem like a local business-to-business show can't compete with the visitor levels of the major shows like the Business Start Up show at Excel or Grand Designs Live (over 100,000 in 2009) with their celebrity endorsement and big budgets, but the stand cost will always be much lower.

At a local show look for who's sponsoring the event and who's speaking – is there a 'local business celebrity' or support from key organisations such as Business Link or your local Chamber of Commerce?

✎ Exercise: Defining your profitable clients: Business-to-Business

Think about your most profitable clients: the ones who value what you do and are prepared to spend what you want to charge. If you can define what characterises them you'll be in with a winning chance of finding plenty more like them at the right exhibition. Take some time to ask yourself the following questions:

- The job they do
- The company they work for/ own
- Size of company
- Industry
- Where they're based
- What motivates them to buy from you?

My profitable clients: Business-to-Consumer

- Age
- Family situation
- Interests, hobbies
- Where they live
- What motivates them to buy from you?

POTENTIAL EXHIBITION CHECKLIST:

- ☐ Location
- ☐ Audience profile
- ☐ Visitor motivation for attending
- ☐ Visitor numbers
- ☐ Size of exhibition
- ☐ Show marketing
- ☐ Sponsorship/ endorsement/ marketing

So you've established that the exhibition visitors are the type of clients you'd like to gain and you can see that the organisers are doing everything they can to promote the show effectively.

Now let's look at how you pick the right stand, then read the exhibitors manual and get your pen and paper out: here's where the fun begins!

CHOOSING THE RIGHT STAND

All stands are not created equal. Some will be in prime positions, others tucked out of the way. If you want to gain hundreds of leads then give yourself a fighting chance and pick a stand that'll benefit from lots of passing traffic. But how do you pick yourself a winner?

LOCATION LOCATION LOCATION.

Contrary to popular belief, the best stands aren't located at the entrance. Visitors want to get into the heart of an exhibition and often rush past these stands. The best place to be is on one of the main thoroughfares near one of the main attractions. See the floorplan example below to see how this works.

SIZE DOESN'T NECESSARILY MATTER

The best stands are usually going to be more expensive. Corner stands and stands near an attraction will command a premium, so sacrifice size over location if you need to. After all, there's no point in having an enormous stand that no one visits!

I'd like to give you an 'ideal' size but it varies so much on what you plan on doing with your stand. I usually take a stand that's 3x4m, which sounds huge, but is actually very small once you're in the space.

As a rule of thumb, as a savvy business owner I'd go for one of the mid-sized stands. The smallest will just make you look mean, and unless you can absolutely afford the biggest and all the posters and literature that goes with it, stick to the mid-size so that you have budget left for all your marketing that goes with this show. The space is just the beginning...

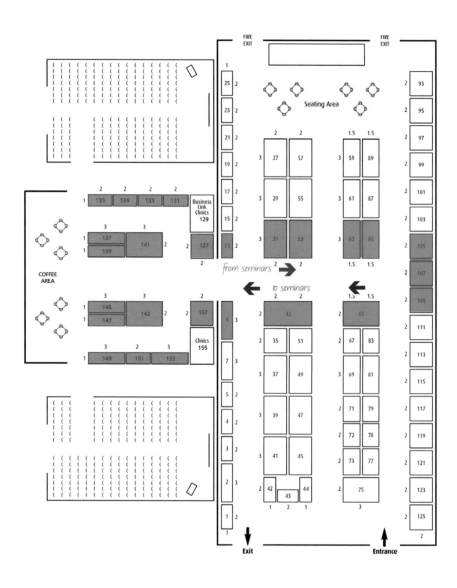

BOOK EARLY FOR THE BEST STAND

When it comes to booking stands there are two strategies that work. Book early to secure the stand of your choice, or book at the absolute last minute (and I mean days before the show) to get a good deal.

Booking at the last-minute will leave you with little time to plan properly so I highly recommend booking early!

HOW TO READ A FLOOR PLAN

There's an art to reading a floor plan, but once you've mastered it it's really not difficult. What you're trying to do is work out which way most of the traffic is going to flow so that you can pick the best spot. You'll also find this knowledge incredibly helpful as we move on to planning the layout of the stand.

Start at the entrance, where are the visitors aiming for? If there's a seminar room they'll probably walk straight to the seminars, similarly if there's a catwalk or show home then that's probably where most visitors will be heading for. How can you make sure they pass your stand?

A stand near the catering area or loos is another good choice as most people have to visit these areas.

At the first exhibition I ever did we were right next to the bar. Aside from the obvious benefits of being next to a bar, it meant that we had a constant supply of visitors standing in a queue looking around at my stand. Fantastic!

Take a look at the floor plan on the opposite page.

Which of the stands do you think are the most attractive? I've shaded the ones I'd pick.

CORNER STANDS

I always encourage my clients to take a corner stand because they're not competing so much for attention with the other stands. You'll also find that they're cheaper to 'dress' as you need fewer posters and you create a more open, relaxed and approachable atmosphere.

AVOID THE SHEEP PENS

Having said size doesn't matter, bear in mind that 2x1m or 2x2m is incredibly small. I'm not too concerned about depth when it comes to a stand, but width is essential to give you a real presence.

DESIGNING YOUR STAND

Designing a stand that will send out the right signals about your business and attract hordes of visitors is no small task. I firmly recommend you find yourself a graphic designer you trust and ask them to help you create some fabulous looking display materials. The look of your stand is too important to try and knock out yourself – you'll just undermine your credibility.

When it comes to designing your stand, whilst creativity is key, we need to start by thinking about how to appeal to the visitors of the show. So let's start by looking at how to understand visitor motivations before we move on to the creative brainstorming around the display materials, furniture and stand layout.

MAKING YOUR BUSINESS IRRESISTIBLE TO THE SHOW VISITORS

If you change just one thing about how you approach exhibitions, change your mindset. I know that up until now we've focused on what you want from the exhibition. Now that you're clear, let's focus on your visitor. How do you make your stand compelling? How do you make your business irresistible?

One of the most powerful things you can do is to stop thinking about what you want to sell people, tell people or sign them up for, and start thinking from the point of view of your visitors.

If you can just switch your focus from what you want to sell to what's motivating your visitors you'll be on the road to success. The challenge is to switch from being inward looking, from thinking about what you want to tell people, to what the visitors want to know.

HOW DO I TAILOR MY OFFERING TO THIS SHOW?

Think about:

- Why visitors are coming to the event
- What are their needs, motivations and problems?
- What solution do you provide to those needs, motivations and problems?

This chapter will help you tailor your offering to the exhibition visitors so that you make it much, much easier for them to buy from you. Let's start by thinking generically about why people are coming to the event.

HOW TO LOOK FOR CLUES AS TO WHY VISITORS ARE COMING

You can use the exhibition marketing materials to gain an insight into the sorts of expectations visitors to the show are going to have on the day. I can't pretend that there isn't an element of educated guesswork here but you can use your industry knowledge, past experience and the exhibition marketing literature to gain a good idea about why people are coming

LOOK AT:

- The exhibition website – what it says and how it looks

- The leaflets

- Any write-ups in trade show or consumer press

- Your experience

- What the organisers say about the show

- The name of the event (often a giveaway!)

The Grand Designs Live website (www.granddesignslive.com) tells me that this is one funky show. Looking at the fonts, colours, imagery and text on the site, as well as my prior understanding of the TV show I am able to draw a conclusion about what the show will be like.

I imagine visitors are coming to gain inspiration, meet new suppliers and understand how they can make their homes more desirable places to live. Some might be coming in the hope of meeting the rather lovely Kevin McCloud too.

These visitors probably pepper their sentences with words like space, dream and eco. They're probably into innovative, technologically advanced, eco-friendly products and they probably read quite trendy and cutting edge magazines. If I were exhibiting at Grand Designs I'd want to choose my most funky, impressive design pieces. I'd also use the same words as the visitors when it came to writing copy. Style is probably more important than budget at this event.

SUCCESSFUL EXHIBITORS TAILOR THEIR OFFERING TO THE SPECIFIC MOTIVATIONS OF VISITORS AT THE SHOW.

Let's take a look at how this works in reality.

As I look through two interior design magazines from the same month, Living Etc and Homes and Gardens, it's interesting to see how a wood burning stove company have selected different products for each magazine. The Living Etc advert has a very sleek, modern, industrial looking stove, whilst Homes and Gardens, which has an older, slightly more suburban readership features a traditional design. What they've done is selected the most appropriate product for the readership of the magazine.

This is exactly what you need to do when it comes to planning your stand. Tailor your message and select products or services that will specifically appeal to the visitors of this event.

By understanding why the visitors are coming to the show and what their problems, needs or motivations are you can match the expectations of the visitors. This is key if you want to achieve maximum impact.

The Designer Wedding show's website talks about

> "Indulging your natural sense of style. About finding every exquisite detail to make your wedding day blissful. Everyone you'll meet at the show has been carefully selected because they share your passion for design, style and luxury."

Wow! And that is exactly what these brides, their mums and their bridesmaids are expecting. A shabby stand that's been poorly put together isn't going to appeal to these style conscious visitors and you'll miss out. No pressure to make your stand exude design, style and luxury then!

GIVING VISITORS WHAT THEY WANT

Try to really get inside the mind of the show visitors and try to empathise with their motivations. If you can do that, then you can directly appeal to them.

People are generally motivated by fear or greed: they're running away from something or towards something. Understanding this means that you'll be able to write copy for your posters, leaflets or emails that directly appeals to your visitors and strikes a powerful chord with them.

Business owners this year might be motivated away from their business going bust and toward financial security or an undisturbed nights' sleep. Prospective brides might be running away from a bland and boring wedding and towards a wedding that people will talk about for years to come.

Once you understand what's motivating someone, you can sell to them effectively. That's easier face to face than when you're preparing in advance, but it's nothing a little insight and experience can't solve.

✏ *Exercise: get focused*

Read through the show literature, website, leaflet, magazine advert: whatever you've got. Make a note of all the key words and phrases that give you clues about what the show is offering

Now get together with a friend or colleague and put yourself into the mind of your target audience. One of you is going to ask the questions and the other is going to be the visitor and provide the answers

- What motivated you to buy tickets/ take time out to attend this exhibition?
- How do you feel at the moment? (Before the event)
- Why do you feel that way?
- How would you like to feel? (After the event)
- What would you like to come away with?

This is a really powerful exercise to help you focus on the needs of your visitors rather than on what you want to sell them. We'll come back to this later on, so keep it safe!

For example...

THE DESIGNER WEDDING SHOW

What motivated you to buy tickets/ take time out to attend this exhibition?	I want to be inspired, I want to meet one of the famous suppliers, for the catwalk show, it looks like a fun day out (and so on...)
How do you feel at the moment?	Overwhelmed at what's out there, unsure about what's out there, unsure about how to create my perfect day, excited about the potential of creating my perfect day
Why do you feel that way?	Because until I got engaged I knew nothing about weddings or how to plan one and I want to get my one special day just right
How would you like to feel?	Inspired and in control
What would you like to come away with?	Plenty of new contacts and ideas

Armed with that insight, if you could tell the show visitors one thing about your business that would solve their problems, what would it be? Can you write one sentence about it?

For example, for Yarwood-White at the Designer Wedding Show the one sentence would probably look something like this:

Award-winning bridal jewellery from Yarwood-White: because details matter.

Take five minutes to write down as many different options as possible. Pick the one you think will most appeal to visitors of your next exhibition.

You're going to use this sentence as your guiding principles. It may appear as your headline on your posters, you might use it in your marketing literature or you may need to tweak it before it goes public. The important thing is that you now have a focus that will directly appeal to the visitors coming to the show.

Now that you've started to think about what your visitors are going to expect of your business and the show, let's move on to thinking about how you'll promote your products and services.

TAILORING YOUR MESSAGE TO THE EVENT

Most businesses sell more than one product or service. This is often because they have multiple target clients, or because the clients might buy more than once. The key to success at an exhibition is to only promote the products or services you feel will solve the problems of the visitors of that specific show.

If you try and promote everything, your stand will look confusing and overwhelming, so stick to a few products or services, and if you really must promote them all, then find a common thread that ties everything together and 'lead' with that.

SOME EXAMPLES AND IDEAS TO GET YOU THINKING.

Type of show	Why are visitors coming?	Company	Focus
Designer wedding show	To gain inspiration about having a stylish wedding	Bridal jeweller	Fashion-led pieces, bespoke jewellery
Print industry show	To see what's new in the industry	Manufacturer of printing presses	The most amazing new piece of equipment you have

Handmade and Vintage Fair	To be inspired for their own crafting and pick up unusual and quirky gifts	Designer-maker	Kits, emphasise handmade
Horticultural show – ie Chelsea, Hampton Court, Tatton Park etc.	To gain ideas, see what's new, meet new suppliers	Gardening magazine	A year of inspiration for just £15

WHAT DO YOU WANT VISITORS TO KNOW, THINK AND DO?

We've established what visitors are expecting to see, and we've also thought about how your business can directly appeal to these people. Let's get back to you and what you want. What do you want visitors to know, think and do? Use this focus to create an effective stand and marketing literature.

GETTING FOCUSED CHECKLIST:

❏ Understand why visitors are coming to the show and match their expectations

❏ Create one sentence that sums up your focus for the show

❏ Work out what you'd like visitors to know, think and do

CREATING YOUR STAND

I hope that this chapter will inspire you to create a stand that will impress potential clients and send out the right signals about your business. You don't need to spend a fortune, just invest a little time, thought and creativity.

The best exhibition stands stop visitors in their tracks. They're impressive, creative, thought provoking and 'on brand'.

Forward planning

When it comes to exhibiting, the further ahead you're able to plan, the better.

You need to think about what's going to appeal to the show's target audience, what promotions you would like and can afford to do, write the copy as well as arrange the graphics and production of your stand materials. Trust me when I tell you that there is a LOT to do!

I recommend you start your planning as soon as you have booked your stand. If you can, allow 2-3 months to create your stand materials and accompanying collateral. You will feel all the less stressed for it, and of course, the finished product will be so much better.

MOMENTS OF TRUTH

First impressions count. Your stand is your shop window for the day. Do it well and you'll attract visitors, show your competitors you mean business and build confidence and trust with your current and potential customers.

But expect to chip up on the day with just a couple of A4 sheets of paper and some product samples and you, and the show visitors, are going to be very underwhelmed.

Like it or not, potential clients will form an impression about your business, positive or negative, based on how your stand looks.

Exhibitions are a Moment of Truth for your business. Your website might look wonderful, your offices an architectural masterpiece and your receptionists' telephone manner exquisite, but if your stand is a mass of unhappy staff and peeling posters then you'll undo all of your hard work.

Every time a customer comes into contact with a part of your organisation, they will form an impression. Jan Carlzon calls these **Moments of Truth**.

If you're serious about your business and your brand then you need to manage each of these moments of truth, or brand touchpoints, and make sure that each of them gives a positive and consistent message about your business.

This means that your stand must be well designed, well laid out, and inviting. It needs to reflect your brand values and support your brand image. Your staff must be smart, welcoming and approachable. And you need to be well organised.

We'll cover stand staff in a later chapter. Let's focus on the stand itself for now.

Create a professional looking stand that has wow factor and it will pay dividends in the long run by sending out the right signals about your business. You simply cannot afford to get this wrong, so pay careful attention to this section if you want to get the right results.

HOW TO BRING YOUR STAND TO LIFE

Exhibitions are live, interactive events that cry out for you to bring your business to life, interact with visitors and create a sensory experience that is unforgettable. It's so simple, and yet so few businesses even attempt to create this experience. I'd like to inspire you to think creatively about how you can bring your business to life and really **make your company stand out from the crowd**.

A recent Holistic and Alternative Therapy show was anything but inspiring. We trudged round the usual uninspiring stands with A4 posters crammed full of text and the obligatory spine model or poster. The cubicles were messy, dull, and far too introverted. But one stand really stood out. The company was demonstrating an unusual type of acupressure that made the patient make a noise as the pressure was applied. Because they'd turned their stand into a bit of a show, they drew a crowd and stood out from all the other dull stands offering their services. Here was a company that understood what visitors would be expecting: to sample holistic therapies, and so they made sure they met that expectation.

The Royal Horticultural Society 'Grow Your Own' weekends are a great example of an organisation bringing their cause to life for multiple audiences. The idea behind the campaign is to get people growing their own fruit and veg.

The RHS had arranged various interactive demonstrations around the garden that really brought growing-your-own to life. There was a series of seminars and a small exhibition as well as goody bags containing 'starter packs' of seeds. They had organised cookery demonstrations and had both experts on hand for those who wanted to develop their knowledge and starter guides for those who had never picked up a trowel. And for the children they had organised tomato planting and a fun show where two characters 'clip' and 'snip', showing the children just how easy it was to grow their own vegetables.

Through careful planning and powerful demonstrations the RHS had successfully demystified vegetable growing and created plenty of enthusiastic gardeners in the process.

HOW CAN YOU BRING YOUR BUSINESS TO LIFE?

Let's imagine you run a Vintage China Hire company. You might just style a beautiful table to show brides what you do. But you could have waitresses serving an afternoon tea to potential customers if you had the space.

You could have posters showing beautiful examples of other weddings you have styled and catered, or you might buy some stunning wallpaper that fits with your brand to create a strong sense of style. I might combine the wallpaper with images in gilt frames if I were doing this for a client.

Here are some other ideas that you could use to bring your business to life. Try and be creative, and think **benefits**! How can what you do benefit the visitors? The bigger the benefit, the bigger the buy-in.

COMPANY	HOW TO BRING IT TO LIFE
HR consultancy	Actors demonstrating typical scenarios and explaining how to deal with them
Make-Up Artist	Makeovers. Portfolio of your work. Plenty of stunning photographs up on the wall.
Image consultant	Demonstrations to 'do your colours' every hour or so
Graphic designer	Slideshow showing plenty of 'before and after's! Take your portfolio along for people to admire.
Web designer	Plasma screen showing a slideshow of websites you're proud of. Perhaps talks on what makes for a successful design or will get your website found.
Solicitor	One-to-one advice sessions – maybe lasting five minutes. At the end, offer to book people for a one hour (perhaps discounted) consultation. Don't forget to take a booking sheet with you!
Accountants	Tax tips sessions – five minutes long or so. Have plenty of printed tips for people to take away with a link to your website or blog where they'll be able to find plenty more.
Studio Photographer	Set up a studio in a portion of your stand and take very quick headshots to sell to visitors
Designer of handmade shoes	Bring your lasts, your fabrics and a pair of half-finished shoes with you and make them whenever you get a moment

Caterer	Give away free samples of your canapés, soup, puddings – whatever will be easy to do and will wow potential clients
Garden designer	Bring your portfolio, some designs you've worked on and perhaps have a video running of some of your best gardens. Consider also bringing some well-planted containers.
Manufacturer of griddle pans	Do a cookery demonstration. Food to taste at the end will always pull the punters in! Don't forget to give away the recipes at the end!

I remember at the franchise exhibition several years ago there were various body-painted actors walking around semi-naked. OK, so they certainly attracted attention! But to be honest, they weren't necessarily appropriate for the event or audience.

DRESS YOUR STAND WITH THINGS THAT BRING YOUR PRODUCT TO LIFE.

I had a fruit theme going on at one exhibition with the strap line 'sharpen up your image'. A tenuous link I know, but it worked! The fruity theme was carried across my website, my stand graphics and also in the sweets –I put out Starburst for hungry visitors. I also filled a glass cube vase with lemons and limes cut in half which gave my stand a really modern, graphical look. It added impact and brought the stand graphics to life.

CREATING A BUZZ

Your stand is your shop window for the day. If it's full of excitement, prospective clients and atmosphere then both you and your clients will go away with a positive impression, so it's essential that you create a buzz.

One of the best ways to do this is with a live demonstration. If you've booked one of the tiny 2x1m stands then you're going to struggle here. But if you have a stand bigger than about 12sq m then you should be OK.

Consider running 5-10 minute demonstrations that will pull in a crowd and bring your product or service to life.

I worked with a web design company who did exactly this. It takes nerve to stand in your space and talk to a handful of people, but a small crowd will draw a bigger crowd, and often by the end of your presentation they'll be clamouring to buy!

OFFER TASTINGS OR SAMPLES

Tastings and samples are the best way to get people to experience what you do and often to buy on the spot, but make sure you don't give away too much.

My cousin runs a Belgian chocolate shop in Orange County, California and often offers tastings in the mall outside her shop. We talked about how this often didn't work for her as people would take the free chocolate but not buy anything. She was giving away a whole Belgian chocolate, which is not only expensive, it satisfies their hunger and removes the need for them to visit the shop to buy anything. By chopping each chocolate into eight pieces visitors have a delicious taste of chocolate in their mouths that they simply have to satisfy – and so they visit the shop and buy not just one, but a whole box to take away for themselves, their friends or their family.

This can work in exactly the same way if you sell consultancy to businesses. Give someone a small taster: a five or ten minute session at the show or a longer (say hour long) session after the exhibition. This whets their appetite, adds value and leaves them wanting more.

INVOLVE ALL THE SENSES

One of the real benefits of an exhibition is that it's live: you can really create a sensory experience for your visitors. How can you involve all five senses: sight, sound, smell, touch and taste?

Products that people can touch, flowers that smell, food for people to taste and music are just some of the ways you can create a sensory experience that brings your business to life.

Be creative, think about the sorts of props that might bring your product to life. If I were designing a stand for the (mythical) Vintage China Hire Company then I would probably buy (or make) some delicious cakes and macaroons to display. And I'd use teapots full of roses draped with pearls and perhaps the odd vintage wedding photograph, and maybe a silver lipstick case and compact to give a real feeling of vintage glamour. You need much more than posters on a stand like this: you need to stage and style to bring the whole concept to life and give visitors a taste of what they can achieve.

Have a brainstorming session with your team, or family and friends if it's just you. How can you bring your business to life?

TECHNICAL CONSIDERATIONS

OK, I'll admit it. This isn't an area that enthrals me. Give me some planning, copywriting or design and I'm happy. I'm ever so slightly suspicious of all things technical. But trust me when I tell you that spending time planning this bit will lift your stand above all the others.

Read the exhibitors manual to see what's included. You would be amazed at how many people don't. It's full of useful stuff, and the sooner you read it, the better!

Every show is different, but turning up on stand build day with your plasma screen, merchant terminal and laptop and finding that there is no power, Internet or lighting supply to your stand is going to cause you a bit of a problem to say the least. Plan all this stuff well in advance, work it into your show budget and order it through the organiser.

USE LIGHTING TO BRING YOUR STAND TO LIFE

Lighting will bring your stand to life. A few well-placed spotlights on your products and headlines will bring them out. Spotlights that clip onto a pop-up scheme are very cost effective and will make a real difference. Bear in mind that if you have lighting you'll also need an electrical socket, so factor the cost of that in as well.

Don't go overboard or your staff will be too hot, unproductive and sweaty. Not a great look.

Consider coloured lights too. Red will evoke hunger, soft blue is considered to be inviting and white will grab attention!

You'll find that if stand lighting isn't included as standard (as it isn't for some shows) that your stand will really stand out amongst all the others. And let's face it. This is what it's all about.

CONSIDER WHETHER YOU'LL NEED AN INTERNET CONNECTION

Having some form of internet connection will probably be a must if you intend on taking a lot of credit card transactions on the day. Find out whether there is a reliable Wifi signal or whether you'll need to make alternative plans. It's also worth remembering that you can take PayPal via your mobile phone now so you may not need an internet connection at all.

If you're going to be demonstrating software then use an offline demo if at all possible. The last thing you want to be doing is apologising for a slow connection.

You can also use the internet as a part of your audio visual, although to be absolutely honest I'd be a little wary of relying on the internet for crucial demonstrations. Past experience (and I'm sure it gets better and better every year) has taught me to be a little suspicious of the speed and reliability of temporary connections.

Look at www.jing.com for software that lets you record what's on your screen - it's ideal for this scenario.

AUDIO VISUAL

Sound is important if you plan on doing a demonstration or presentation on your stand. Exhibition Audio Visual companies can set up a sound system and microphone that won't intrude too much on your neighbours. Naturally if you have a 2x1m stand then this type of equipment is slightly over the top! But for larger stands it's an absolute must. Not only will AV enable you to be heard, it will also draw in a crowd clamouring to hear your expert opinions!

Video and slideshow demonstrations can be a great way to draw people on to your stand. It's also a great excuse to buy an enormous plasma screen on the company!

Consider using a giant plasma screen to showcase:

* A portfolio of your work
* Testimonials from clients if you can get them to be interviewed!
* A video about your business
* Key facts or statistics
* A sales presentation
* Information
* Your product being used

Don't forget to keep it simple. And keep it short work on a continuous loop of about 3 minutes, no longer as people won't want to hang around for hours at the edge of your stand.

FURNITURE

It's easy to forget about furniture when it comes to planning your stand, but there are two reasons to think about this early on. Firstly, ordering your furniture late usually means you pay a surcharge, which you'll want to avoid. And secondly, you need to think about your stand as a whole. Not just in terms of the posters, but what's going to go on the stand and how your promotional literature will fit around that.

Knowing the type of furniture you're going to need goes back to thinking about how you're going to use the stand. Go back to your objectives. Do you want to 'touch' your leads quickly with a quick smile and a few pleasantries? Or do you plan to have a long consultation with people? I'd recommend you only have long consultations with people if you have a large salesforce on the stand and if you're selling big, expensive products.

I find that the most profitable way of exhibiting is to use the day to build my database and gain quality leads. If I think back to all the exhibitions I've worked on, I honestly feel that in every case, the consultative sales would have been better focused on back in the office. So the need for a consultation area won't be essential for most businesses.

Your exhibitor manual will usually contain details of the official furniture supplier and that's one easy option, but don't forget that this is not your only source of furniture. Be creative and source pieces that are on-brand and add to the experience you're trying to create on your stand. You can always source furniture from your home, friends homes, antique fairs, DIY centres and (a favourite of mine!) Auctions and car boot sales.

CHOOSE FURNITURE THAT WORKS WITH YOUR STAND DESIGN AND FITS WITH YOUR COMPANY BRAND.

When I kitted out our new office I chose lots of brightly coloured office chairs as well as investing in some designer chairs for the meeting room. They were impactful, interesting and most certainly on brand.

It's the same with your stand furniture. Exhibition furniture hire companies have a pretty wide range of colours and styles these days, so try and avoid the bog standard and let your personality and your brand values shine through. Consider using your own furniture where possible.

For example, a company hiring vintage china for weddings and baby showers could use an old welsh dresser or a dark-wood antique chest or bookshelves to display their product on. And the chairs might be wrought iron garden chairs with kitsch vintage cushions on them?

If your company is a firm of solicitors and your corporate colours are blue and red, why not order blue and red topped bar stools, rather than the normal chrome chairs? The point is to have your furniture complement your stand design, your brand and your product, rather than looking like an afterthought.

SEATING

Sitting down at exhibitions never looks great. But if, like me, you like to wear high heels then you'll need some form of support for your poor legs, back and feet by the end of the day. I like to order bar stools to lean back against. You're still at eye level, and to be honest, during the manic part of an exhibition (usually 10.45-2.15pm) you probably won't go anywhere near them. But towards the end of the day they are an absolute godsend. I was five months pregnant at my last event and I spent most of the day perched on that bar stool.

Every year I consider buying bar stools as they cost almost as much to hire as they do to buy. But every year I remind myself that I'm still waiting for the dream kitchen to put them in. Next year Rodders, next year!

If you're going to do some more consultative selling you'll need something a bit more comfortable than a bar stool. Sofas are often a little too intimate for you both to perch on. How about some chairs and a table?

TABLES, DESKS AND PLINTHS

I recommend my clients use a branded plinth to display their competition poster (we cover this later) and container on as well as using it for the giveaways. You may also need furniture for your computers and breakfast-bar-height plinths to display products on.

DISPLAYING YOUR PRODUCTS

If you have physical products to display then you need to think carefully about display systems that will show off your products in the best possible light. A company that manufactures or sells promotional products, branded pens and mugs etc might find that a Perspex display system made of clear cubes works well. It would show off the products in the best light and probably need no bells and whistles.

If you're selling something more traditional then you may need something less contemporary. Bridal jeweller Yarwood-White uses glass-fronted bookcases to display their jewellery. And this year at the Designer Wedding show they added vintage teacups, cake stands and mirrors to set off their Modern Heirloom collection. In this case it's about creating a feel, a lifestyle and you need more than stark Perspex boxes to do that. You can see more in the case study at the back of this book.

DISPLAYING YOUR LITERATURE

Will you have literature on the edge of your stand for people passing by to take? Or will you only hand over your prized brochure once you've captured your prospect's details? I would recommend that you have plenty of low cost literature that is in easy reach of everyone, and then hold back your more expensive collateral for the follow up of your hottest prospects.

You'll need to put some very specific, offer/ discount-based show leaflets on the edge of the stand for interested parties to take, so plan on having some form of display stand – whether it's a carrier bag stand, a Perspex leaflet dispenser or one of those metal literature holders. And as one of your show objectives is to raise awareness of your company, you're going to want as many people walking around with your literature as possible.

You can only physically speak to so many people in a day, so the more people that take your literature away, the better. You also need to bear in mind that there are a lot of shy people about who just don't want to talk to you. So if you insist on capturing data before you give anything away, then who's losing out? It will be you as well as the visitor!

CARRIER BAGS

I always give away carrier bags at an exhibition. There are a lot of visitors who love to pick up as many freebies as possible, so having a big, bright, branded carrier bag ensures that it's my logo that's being walked around the exhibition hall.

No one could accuse carrier bags of being the cheap option, so if you are going to give out carrier bags make sure that yours are bigger and better than everyone else's. If yours are the biggest and strongest then yours will be the one that all the other bags get put inside, resulting in maximum exposure for you.

I'd recommend you put your bags at the edge of your stand on a carrier bag holder for people to help themselves to. If what's in your bags is particularly desirable or expensive then you might like to have them towards the back of the stand and ask people to fill out a form or leave their business card with you. If you do this then you'll need to make sure you have plenty on display to entice people on to the stand.

The English Garden magazine did this very well at the Chelsea Flower Show. They were offering a great rate on subscriptions at the show in return for a free book and some free seeds in a very nice bag. Their posters detailed the subscription offering, had images of previous front covers and visuals of the seeds. They had then lined up bags on their counter and had plenty of magazines out for visitors to leaf through. It was a very effective stand.

LOCKABLE STORAGE

If you're attending a show over multiple days you'll need to think about building some secure storage on to your stand. You'll need to take real valuables, like your laptop, off site every night, but if you have products that you'd like to keep safe from prying hands when your stand is unattended, then you'll need a cupboard or suchlike that can be locked.

FRIDGES, COFFEE MACHINES AND REFRESHMENTS

If you have a large stand it can be a nice idea to provide your visitors with some kind of hospitality. Coffee machines, fridges with drinks in and sweet dispensers are all nice ideas. Do be aware that coffee machines are ten a penny at many shows, and they do encourage people to stop and chat for a long time, so only include them if they fit with your show objectives.

FURNITURE LIST:

You might need some, or all, of the following

- ☐ Bar stools
- ☐ Chairs
- ☐ Sofa
- ☐ Side tables
- ☐ Table
- ☐ Counter
- ☐ Display cabinets
- ☐ Carrier bag stands
- ☐ Literature display stands
- ☐ Lockable storage

CREATING AN IMPACT

Think of a trade show and more often than not you'll conjure up an image of a shell scheme with plain, grey walls punctuated with the odd small poster jammed full of black text. A couple of black (or worse, grey) suited and booted smart looking staff sitting behind a municipal looking table full of literature and the obligatory bowl of Celebrations complete the picture. Hardly inspiring is it?

A professional looking, eye-catching stand is absolutely essential for making sure that you stand out, generate trust and create interest on the day. Treat your stand space like a theatre – dress it well for impact!

You'll need to allow enough time and budget to do this properly. I often speak to people who say… "I've spent £2000 on the stand, I can't afford to spend more than £200 on posters". Quite frankly, if that's the case then you should have gone for a smaller stand. The stand space just gets you in, you have got to make it look fantastic to attract the right number of visitors and make the whole thing worthwhile.

As a rule of thumb I'd recommend you spend at least the same amount on your posters and marketing literature as you have on your stand. In reality this might need to be two or three times as much. Do remember that much this can be re used.

PLANNING YOUR POSTERS

Even if you don't use posters to cover your entire stand, you'll need some posters with some attention-grabbing headlines to draw people in and show them how you can help them.

Remember that exercise we did at the start of this section where we thought about what visitors would be expecting and how you could solve their problems? Well it's time to bring out your notes again.

You're going to need to create at least one poster to stop people in their tracks, and ideally another to explain how you solve their problems. Let's see how that works.

CAPTURE PEOPLE'S ATTENTION – AND FAST!

You have less than three seconds to capture the attention of passing visitors or you've lost them. And you'll need to work hard to get people to stop in their tracks. Literally. To stop people passively walking past your stand you'll need a compelling message, a beautiful product or an amazing spectacle to get them to slow down and look closer.

WRITING HEADLINES THAT GET PEOPLE TO STOP

You're working here at two levels: conscious and subconscious. The subconscious mind works in a nanosecond to help the visitor decide whether to give your stand even a microsecond of consideration. At a subconscious level you'll need to think about bright colours, smells or movement. And that's why small posters on grey walls don't work: they just don't register.

At a more conscious level let's think back to people's motivations of fear and greed. Competitions, giveaways, food are all great ways to capture someone's attention. I always position a large poster into the traffic flow with the something enticing, At our last local show I used the headline **"Win a brand makeover worth £1013"**. We picked up 191 leads: almost 25% of the total show visitors.

The side walls are generally where you'll put something to grab attention. Usually I'll put a 'can't-miss-it' competition here, but headlines like **"bunions gone forever"** (assuming that's your business) or **"8 hours sleep a night- guaranteed"** at a baby show are great attention grabbers. You might put an amazing offer like **"iPhones from £10 a month"** or **"3 issues for just £1"** or you might run a competition like **"win a year's supply of wine"** or **"win a luxury holiday to Barbados"**.

Whatever you choose to put on the walls, you're going to need posters of some description that show:

- Your company logo
- An attention grabbing headline, offer or competition
- How you solve the visitors problems
- What you want people to do

Flujo specialise in home working solutions and were exhibiting at a local business to business show. We created posters that were large photographs of a beautiful home office. David the MD brought along a desk, chair and stationery to bring the 'home office' to life and then we had hanging signs with information about how Flujo could help the show visitors. The posters contained headlines like "better home working" and "what are your homeworking challenges" which encouraged visitors to stop and chat to the stand staff. For Flujo, this exhibition was as much about getting frontline feedback as it was selling products.

So the question is, what do you put on your posters? Space will dictate what you can do to a certain extent, and remember that less is often more.

HOW TO CREATE POSTERS WITH PUNCH

I'm starting with the assumption that you're probably going to be planning and creating your posters yourself with the help of your trusted Graphic Designer. Here are my golden rules:

START WITH A SINGLE ANGLE OR PROPOSITION.

Think back to your planning. What do you want people to know, think and do? How can you communicate that effectively? Remember people are unlikely to stop and read everything on your posters so avoid the temptation to fill them with lots of copy. Striking images and one sentence is the way to go. Ideally use that sentence we created at the beginning of this chapter.

MAKE SURE YOUR POSTERS MAKE AN IMPACT IN THE SPACE.

A big space calls for big, bold posters, preferably that cover the walls. Avoid small, self-printed posters (unless you're a printer), they just look messy. Your graphics need to be clean, simple and eye catching. Work with a graphic designer to make them look professional. It will make such a difference to the way you're perceived.

Think about how people will approach your stand when planning your posters. Put the most important information, your headline or your offer, on the wall that people will look directly into. In other words, when you sketched the traffic flow onto the floor plan it'll be the poster that faces the traffic flow.

USE HEADLINES TO DRAW PEOPLE IN.

Think about drawing attention to your offer or competition, or challenging them with a statement like "How Would You Like to Double Your Net Profits This Year?" It's hard to walk past posters like that isn't it?

Keep body copy short and sweet. No one is going to stand there and read paragraphs of text. To be honest I am very against any body copy on stand posters: in reality your posters are just branded wallpaper. Use bullets if you absolutely must!

PUT COPY AT EYE LEVEL OR ABOVE OR IT WILL GET LOST.

Remember that people are looking at your stand from a distance and your posters are often going to be obscured by other people on the stand, so make sure your headlines are high enough for people to see but not so high that they get obscured by the fascia (which usually comes down to 2m).

MAKE SURE YOUR STAND CLEARLY TELLS VISITORS ABOUT WHAT YOU'RE OFFERING.

You've got less than three seconds to convince a passer by to stop at your stand. The headline will draw them in, and next they're thinking "Well, what is this business? How can it help me?". And this is where your posters and product displays will really come into their own. If you're an author promoting your book on bird watching, tell them in huge letters on the back wall! Don't just rely on your tiny A5 book displayed on a plinth to do the job for you. Grab attention and generate interest with your posters.

FIND A WAY TO COVER UP THE SHELL SCHEME

The first step to creating a stand with wow factor is to make sure you cover up the shell scheme. With the exception of shows with black shell schemes, the grey walls have to be some of the most uninspiring spaces, and when you're walking around hundreds of stands it gets tiresome. If you want to stand out, you need to cover up the walls.

You don't have to cover your stand with posters, nor do you need to spend an absolute fortune. **Be creative:** try wallpaper, fabric – even brown paper if it fits with your brand (it could look fabulous on a florists' stand!). You could paint MDF or plywood with a beautiful colour or just use white lining paper. It will make such a difference.

GETTING PEOPLE ONTO YOUR STAND

Attracting the maximum amount of people onto your stand is key to ensuring that you capture leads and build your database. And whilst this focus runs very much throughout the book here are some specific ideas you might find helpful.

USE YOUR CLIENTS AS ADVOCATES.

You might do this informally, by asking clients if they would be happy to chat to a stand visitor, when this feels appropriate. The other alternative, which I think is very smart, is to actually recruit a client to come and work with you on your stand for the day.

Matt Pereira, wedding and lifestyle photographer, asked one of his brides to work with him on his stand at the National Wedding Show. The bride attracted a lot of attention in her wedding dress and was the ideal advocate for Matt. Even better, Matt had taken along the bride's wedding album so that prospective clients could get a feel for the work he did.

INVITATION ONLY

If you promote your attendance well at the show then you'll probably find there are plenty of friendly faces visiting you throughout the day. Why not invite them to an on-stand drinks reception? I know of one company that created an entirely enclosed stand and handed out invitations to join the stand staff for a drink at specific times. It worked exceptionally well.

I'm not sure about closing off your stand entirely, but I would advocate having a reception on your stand.

BOOK SALES SLOTS.

Offering your clients or prospective clients the chance to pre-book a sales slot is a great way to ensure your stand is always busy. Make sure you have enough space and enough staff to be able to do this, and be realistic about how much time you can give to each person.

A similar option is to offer a 'surgery' or Q&A session. Again, you'll need to pre-book this, so ensure you have enough resources and make some space for it. I'd recommend 10 minute slots, and certainly no more than half an hour. Give yourself adequate time between each slot and don't over run!

KEEP YOUR STAND BUSY AT ALL TIMES

No one likes to walk into an empty restaurant and feel the waiters are ready to pounce on them at any point. It's the same with an empty stand. Use the show as an opportunity to network and build relationships: with other exhibitors if things are really quiet. Ask questions, encourage conversation, share your expertise and you'll find you won't be lonely for long.

PLANNING OUT THE SPACE

Having an overall plan of how you're going to use your stand is your starting point when it comes to creating visuals. Start by thinking about the space you have.

You'll need to consider:

- The **size** of your stand?
- How many **sides** does it have? Is it a corner stand, open on three sides or enclosed on three sides?
- Which way will the **traffic flow** past the stand?
- Which is the **'key wall'** for getting people to stop?

Think about what needs to be in that space:

- Your product (if you have one)
- Display cabinets if necessary
- Furniture
- Storage space if it's a long show or a large stand

Bear in mind that **spaces always feel smaller when you get there on the day**. It's worth mocking up your stand if you're not used to exhibiting. Mark out the space on the floor (with newspapers or masking tape – I'm not suggesting you spray-paint your new carpets!) and if you can, use a corner of your room and enclose the space with a pop-up stand or piece of card, wallpaper, whatever you have to hand. Use anything that will give you a 3 dimensional view of the space you have to work with. If in doubt, under rather than over-furnish your stand as it looks better. White space is a wonderful thing and that concept works for interiors as well as on paper.

STOPPING THE TRAFFIC RIGHT OUTSIDE YOUR STAND.

Want to get visitors to stop at your stand? Then we need to think about how they approach your stand as they walk around the exhibition. I'm going to show you how to use the floorplan and your knowledge of the visitor flow around the exhibition to maximise the potential of your stand.

Let's start by having a look at my stand from the Grow Your Business exhibition last year.

THE FLOOR PLAN.

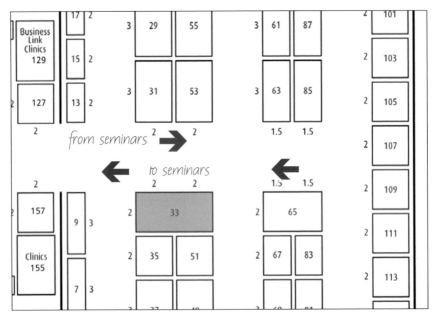

My stand is the one shaded. The arrows represent the flow of traffic to and from the seminars. This is important because the vast majority of visitors will be attending at least one seminar, so we know which way the traffic is flowing. For the full floor plan see the section on Reading a Floor Plan.

MARKING ON THE KEY WALLS

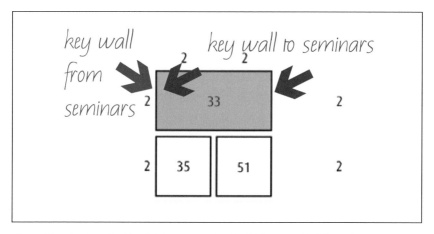

Above: The stand marked in pink is an open stand, which means that the only wall is at the back (bottom of the picture). The rest of the sides are completely open. This gives me maximum flexibility in terms of what I place where.

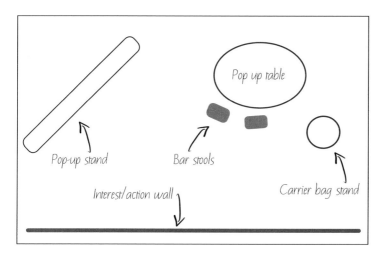

LAYING OUT THE FURNITURE

I played about with options for placing furniture before deciding on the layout above.

✏️ Creating a stand plan

You'll need to get a copy of the exhibition floorplan, which you'll usually find on the exhibition website if you don't have it to hand.

Take a new sheet of paper and sketch out your stand. Add the dimensions and try and get it (roughly) to scale. Highlight the walls.

Next you'll need to mark on the traffic flow with an arrow. To do this you'll need to be able to read the floor plan, so take a look at the section earlier in this chapter.

If you struggle with working out where the traffic is going to be flowing then ask the organisers for help. They'll be happy to help you: after all, they want this to be a great show for you so that you'll re-book for next year, so it's in their interests to give you as much help as they can.

Plan your posters for maximum impact. Highlight the wall that most of the traffic is going to see first – your "attention" wall, and mark your "interest/ action" wall (usually the back wall) which is where visitors will look next once you've stopped them in their tracks

Finally place your furniture.

CHECKLIST:

- ☐ Think creatively about how you'll use the space
- ☐ Create a stand with impact
- ☐ Work with a graphic designer to create professional looking, clutter free posters
- ☐ Cover up the shell scheme

SPEAKING & SEMINARS

Presenting a workshop or seminar is an effective way to really make a show work for you.

Many exhibitions use seminars to attract visitors, and if you get in quickly enough you may be able to secure yourself a speaking slot. Running a seminar gives you instant credibility. You gain the opportunity to demonstrate your skills in front of a group of people who all need your help and chances are, if your seminar is good, you'll gain plenty of business.

Public speaking isn't for everyone but if you're a confident and practiced speaker and have the opportunity to speak on a topic you're a true expert in then it can really work for you.

When you're looking at a show, ask the organisers about any seminars they're running and whether there are any opportunities. Then follow up immediately with a speaker sheet.

The organisers will usually outline what they'd like you to cover. Make sure you talk about things that will really add value to the audience.

Don't try and turn it into a 45 minute advert for your business, or you'll seriously put off any potential clients. Instead, give as much information as you possibly can, be enthusiastic and at the end your audience will be receptive to a 60 second plug. I've found from experience that the most powerful plugs are to invite people to join my mailing list and to enter our competition.

✏️ Creating a speaker sheet

Exhibition organisers are always inundated with requests from enthusiastic exhibitors and non-exhibitors hoping to boost their exposure by speaking. They can't say yes to everyone, so they tend to go with the best speakers who know their stuff and will probably attract the most visitors.

Usually event organisers will invite speakers they've seen before and they know are good. But if you haven't had exposure to these people, create a 'speaker sheet' that will put you ahead of the game. Here's how to do it.

- ☐ Create a seminar title that will attract attention
- ☐ Add a sub heading: how to... five simple steps... how you can...
- ☐ Write an introductory paragraph: why is your seminar so essential to the exhibition visitors?
- ☐ Outline what your seminar will cover
- ☐ Explain how the audience will benefit
- ☐ Add a testimonial from someone who has attended/ booked you for a seminar before (this will add reassurance that you know what you're doing)
- ☐ Put on a photograph
- ☐ Add some background information about you and what qualifies you to speak on the subject
- ☐ Don't forget your contact details!
- ☐ Make sure it's well designed and create PDF that you can email across at a moment's notice.

SPEAKER SHEETS SHOW YOU MEAN BUSINESS!

Speaker sheets show that you're a serious speaker as well as also saving the organisers the hassle of thinking of seminar topics. I have six or seven different speaker sheets and I also email them to organisations I think might be interested in booking me. I have a 95% success rate so far with them! I hope they work for you.

PREPARE CHEAT SHEETS AND HANDOUTS FOR THE SEATS

If you get a coveted speaker slot, maximise your exposure by creating 'cheat sheets' or handouts to put on the seats. Create a simple, well-branded leaflet or flyer that gives people five steps, or twelve steps or whatever to success with your chosen subject.

Make sure it looks great, and don't forget to include your contact details on there. You'll probably also want to create a 'product' such as a one to one session at a special price that people can take advantage of later.

And one more thing... Have your cheat sheet proof read by someone independent, preferably a professional. I still cringe when I think of my first big speaking gig. I created some fabulous looking handouts, nervously presented my seminar and somehow got to the end. I was feeling pretty good... until someone gave me my cheat sheet back with all my grammatical errors marked up. I was mortified. It completely ruined the rest of my day. Needless to say he didn't want to work with me!

WHAT IF I DON'T GET TO SPEAK?

My experience as an exhibitor, and also as the seminar planner for Grow Your Business is that a large proportion of exhibitors who would like to speak do not get the opportunity. This is often not a personal thing: certain topics are more hotly sought after than others and many organisers will favour a speaker with a track record over one without.

So what do you do if you don't get to speak? The real benefit of speaking at an exhibition or conference is that you raise your profile, share your expertise and develop a relationship with a very targeted audience. If you don't get to speak you need to get creative and find ways of doing that.

Why not explore whether there is an opportunity to write an article for the event show guide or blog? Perhaps you can find creative ways of giving away expert tips from your stand?

There's also nothing to stop you presenting a very short seminar (five minutes or so) from your stand. Do check with the event organisers but most will be amenable to this, so long as you control the sound and don't annoy your fellow exhibitors.

Remember too that it's what you do after the event that really matters in building relationships. We'll look at how you do that in the final part: after the exhibition.

PRE-EVENT PUBLICITY

Given that most visitors arrive at an exhibition with a fixed agenda it's important that you publicise your company effectively before the day if you're to get the most out of the event.

MAXIMISE YOUR BRAND EXPOSURE

To get the very best out of your next event you need to let your potential clients know that you're going to be at the show, and that you have something very valuable to offer them. Pre-event publicity will help you create a real buzz and help you get on to that all-important agenda. Here's how.

WRITE 100 WORDS OR SO ABOUT YOUR BUSINESS FOR THE SHOW GUIDE.

At every exhibition there will be a show guide. Write some copy in plenty of time that promotes your business effectively. Make sure you:

- ☐ Keep to the point

- ☐ Stick to the word limit (you don't want some ham-fisted organiser cutting down your words!)

- ☐ Include details of your show offer

- ☐ Explain concisely why visitors to the show must visit your stand

- ☐ Give details of any special freebies or giveaways on your stand

Get this right and you'll find that you attract more visitors to your stand on the day, as well as generating more enquiries after the event. I found that at my very first exhibition I had people walking onto the stand saying, "You were on my list of people to visit". How wonderful is that? I'd been in business all of a day, and already people were starting to notice us!

SUBMIT ARTICLES OR BLOGS TO THE ORGANISERS TO BOOST YOUR BRAND PRESENCE AT THE SHOW

Many exhibition organisers are wising up to the fact that keeping in touch with visitors via a blog can help gain visitors, generate interest in the show and build relationships before the event has happened. If your next exhibition has a blog or perhaps a newsletter then take advantage of it!

Being featured on an event blog will not only boost your brand awareness, but will also start the all-important process of positioning yourself as an expert. If you currently have your own blog then finding material will be easy. If you haven't published anything before then don't worry. Here are some useful ideas to help you:

- Top Tips
- Ten ways you can... save money/ grow your profit/ boost your brand presence/ get your book published/ have a stylish wedding/ make your home eco friendly/ save energy/ lose weight... or whatever your business does.
- 100-500 words on something you're passionate about at the moment
- A case study

Whatever you choose, remember: **keep it objective.** If you turn it into a sales pitch then you'll lose credibility and risk not getting your article published. You'll also alienate visitors before you've even started.

Keep it useful, full of helpful hints and wise words that will have people flocking to come and speak to you! Finish the article with a sentence or two that includes a link to your website, how you help your clients and which stand you'll be on. For example, *John Smith is a Chiropractor based in Lingfield and will be at the Local Business Expo showing you some simple desk exercises you can do to keep your back healthy. Meet him and the team on stand 142.*

PROMOTE YOUR PROMOTIONS

Tell the organisers about any competitions, big discounts, demonstrations or offers you'll be promoting on the day. Do you plan on running a fabulous competition, a special show offer or discount for visitors? Will you be having someone slightly famous (yes, that includes you if you do a lot of public speaking!) doing a demonstration or talk on your stand?

Organisers will love the fact that you're giving away a big prize or discount: it gives them something else to talk about, and it will encourage more visitors to the event. The chances are, if it's a big enough prize or offer and you tell them about it early enough, that they will want to include this in their promotions.

CONSIDER GOODY BAGS

Almost every exhibition gives out branded goody bags on the door. Putting inserts into these bags is a great way to boost your exposure and ensure that everyone takes home some information about your company, even if you don't get to speak to them on the day. You may also be able to sponsor the bags themselves and get your logo on the outside of every bag walking round the event.

Generally more than 80% of visitors will take an official show goody bag, which should increase your exposure. When I create bags for my own stand I usually make up about 15% of anticipated visitor numbers.

If you're going to put inserts into the goody bags then normal promotional rules apply: your insert must be relevant, well designed, and pass the three second rule. More on that later. Anything quirky, creative and that gets your business noticed is generally a good bet.

HAVE PEOPLE WALKING AROUND HANDING OUT YOUR GOODIES

You'll never manage to pull every single visitor onto your stand unless it's a very small show. Having some of your team roaming around with branded goodies gives you a second chance to increase your exposure and encourage more people to visit you.

Consider handing out refreshments as people come out of seminars. Branded bottles of water, fruit and sweets work well, what could you use?

INVITE YOUR CLIENTS.

It's easy to think that marketing the exhibition is solely the role of the Exhibition Organiser. However, when exhibitors get involved in promoting their attendance at a show, wonderful things start to happen.

Promoting your attendance at a show will encourage your tribe to connect with you on neutral territory. It's a great opportunity to build relationships, make new connections and explore opportunities.

SPREADING THE WORD COST-EFFECTIVELY:

- Put leaflets or flyers in with your **invoices** or products, perhaps with a handwritten compliments slip telling people "We'll be on Stand X, look forward to seeing you there!"
- Take the leaflets to **networking events**
- Put a **poster** up in your shop window or reception area
- Put a link to the show in your **email signature**
- Send out **email invitations** to your database
- Mention the event and your giveaway or show offer in your **newsletters** – ideally every one from now till the event.
- **Tweet** about it and mention in social networking forums
- Talk about it at **60-second style networking** events.
- Put the event on your **website and blog**

LITERATURE & GIVEAWAYS

Around two thirds of all literature picked up at a show is likely to hit the recycling bin as soon as visitors return to their home or office so it's important that the literature you create for the show is both impressive and relatively inexpensive. The more compelling and relevant your literature the more likely it is to stay in the 'keep' pile.

I'd recommend you create some inexpensive literature for handing out indiscriminately and then have something more elaborate that you can mail to qualified leads after the exhibition.

PLANNING YOUR PROMOTIONAL MATERIALS

Let's split the literature you'll need into several sections to make things easier when it comes to planning. You will need literature:

- To **give away** at the event
- To **follow up** with immediately after the event
- To **keep in touch** with your newly boosted database for a long time after the event

As a rule of thumb, I would say that most exhibitors would need a very specific show leaflet or flyer with a small-ish proportion of some chunkier brochures that you'll send out after the event.

EXHIBIT! HOW TO USE EXHIBITIONS TO GROW YOUR BUSINESS

LEAFLETS

You need something that looks great, feels good, but is low cost enough to distribute with abandon. Something like an A5 leaflet or flyer is probably ideal, perhaps a folded leaflet if you have a lot of information to get across.

Think about:

- Who is it for? Why do they need my services/ product?
- How are they feeling right now and how can I help?
- Why is my company relevant to visitors to this show?
- What do you want people to know, think and do?

USE AIDCA TO CREATE A STRONG STRUCTURE.

AIDCA stands for Attention, Interest, Desire, Conviction and Action and it's a great tool starting point for creating powerful copy and an effective piece of marketing literature.

Here's how it works:

Attention: Are you talking to me?

Capture attention with a powerful headline and strong design (within three seconds) or your leaflet will go in the bin.

Interest: Why are you talking to me, what do you want me to know?

Think hard about why your prospective customer needs what you're selling: make it relevant, put yourself in their shoes.

Desire: It's a nice idea but do I really want it or need it?

Be persuasive, show how others have benefitted, sell the sizzle!

Conviction: Hmmm, sounds good but how can I be sure I'm not making a mistake?

Use testimonials, reviews, guarantees and a great design to reassure your customer they are in safe hands.

Action: What do I need to do now?

Create a clear, simple and prominent call to action.

EXHIBIT! HOW TO USE EXHIBITIONS TO GROW YOUR BUSINESS

It's a good idea to create an irresistible, time-bound and incredibly prominent offer to encourage an influx of immediate sales. As well as an amazing Buy It Today type of offer, you may want to consider a smaller offer if people order within a couple of weeks.

How about inviting the visitor to check out your website and download a special How To... guide or Top Tips booklet? Ask them to sign up to your database when they visit your website, then not only will you be able to track how many people are downloading your guides, you'll also capture leads from people that you may not have spoken to on the day.

A SHOW-SPECIFIC WEB PAGE

You might like to consider setting up a web page specifically for the show visitors. The idea is that you create something highly relevant to the show and might include special offers, downloads, and details of any competitions you're running on the day. Use a URL shortener service like bit.ly or tinyurl to keep it nice and short, or splash out on an intuitive domain name.

A 'HOW TO...' GUIDE

Checklists, action plans, 'how to' guides, 7 ways you can... and so on are invaluable to give away at an exhibition. They cost virtually nothing to produce and yet are incredibly useful to visitors. Consider the sorts of challenges your prospective clients are facing and what tips you can provide to help with that. For example:

- 7 ways to network more effectively
- 5 steps to looking fabulous on your wedding day
- How to create professional-looking stationery
- Your thirteen step action plan to making your home more energy efficient
- How to grow tomatoes without a greenhouse
- How to get your children interested in fruit and vegetables
- 19 steps to tweeting your business to profit!

HOW TO PRODUCE YOUR 'HOW TO' GUIDES

You can either give these away as hard copies from your stand, or create a series of automated emails or downloadable PDF that your visitors can sign up to from your website.

The benefit of giving them away on the day is that you will probably distribute more. The whole point of doing this sort of exercise is to demonstrate your expertise, and so the more people you give your tips to, the better. The downside of giving away your tips on the day is that they might get lost amongst the plethora of stuff that visitors have collected. You also risk de-valuing these tips slightly if you're just handing them out willy-nilly!

GIMMICKS & FREEBIES

Whether you choose to invest in any branded promotional items is entirely down to you. Many exhibitors see pens, mugs, baseball caps, squishy balls and so on as an exhibitor's necessity, but it's hard to justify the expense in a recession. It's certainly true that branded items will remind the client about your business. It's also true that visitors of exhibitions love, and expect, freebies. So the chances are you'll want to give away something: the question is - what?

Be creative. You don't have to go for the standard branded pen/ post-it/ memory stick/ teddy bear option. How can you tie-in what your business does with the exhibition?

At the Chelsea Flower show many exhibitors give away packets of seed. This might not be wholly original, but it's certainly relevant, interactive and a great keepsake.

A private GP practice was giving away apples at an exhibition last year which I thought was a genius idea. An 'apple a day keeps the doctor away' after all. And it was nice to pick something up other than sweets and chocolates for a change.

If you're going to give away food, then make sure it's individually wrapped. The thought of 200 grubby mitts all over your mint imperials? Eurgh!   I suppose this is why Celebrations and Miniature Heroes are incredibly popular. But they are a little predictable aren't they?

Try and think of something more interesting if you can. Here are some ideas:

- Fruit
- Personalised cookies or cupcakes
- Chocolates
- A bag of sweets in colours that reflect your brand with your business card inside
- A flower or plant
- Bottled water, labelled with your brand and contact details.
- Branded takeaway coffee cups
- Canvas or strong card carrier bags: make them look so beautiful that people want to carry them around

GOODY BAGS

Goody bags can be pricey but they are great for boosting your brand exposure. If this is a route you go down invest in strong, big, and well branded bags, so that it's your bag that visitors stuff the rest of their bags into.

Think about popping in your 'how to' guides as well as sales leaflets, business cards and any other quirky treats you have in mind.

THE GLOSSY BROCHURE

The days of a glossy brochure being part of every business owners' arsenal are pretty much over now aren't they? Websites have long since replaced printed literature and you may find that you just don't need a traditional 'leave behind'.

I'd urge you to think about what you can do to really make your business stand out, and for me, nothing beats a bit of good old fashioned snail mail. A well executed brochure, gift pack or even set of postcards will set you apart from the competition and really show that you're worth doing business with.

You'll find that conversion rates increase dramatically when you send something with real thought and care. What would work for your business?

Whatever you choose, take the time to create something memorable and that has real value. Don't hand them out at the show, instead surprise your prospective customers with them after a productive conversation.

CAPTURE DATA

Capturing data is at the heart of a successful exhibition. And the more you can capture, the better. Now there are just two caveats to that. You must capture relevant, meaningful data. And of course, you must do something with it afterwards!

RUN A COMPETITION TO CAPTURE LEADS

Running a competition is the best way to capture hundreds of leads to build your database with. Give away a big-ticket, irresistible prize that will have visitors flocking to your stand to enter the competition.

I usually give away a branding makeover worth over £1000 which includes a new corporate identity and a stationery pack for the winning business owner. I create an enormous poster to advertise it, put a smaller poster in front of a vase on a plinth, and invite people to drop their business cards in to enter the competition. It always works and we usually get in excess of 100 business cards. At one exhibition this year we left with 191 cards: not a bad result!

Having 100 business cards is all very well, but you won't gain any work from these leads if they aren't interested in your company. And that's why giving away bottles of champagne, doughnuts or iPads doesn't win you any business – unless of course your company sells those things.

If you give away a random prize like doughnuts or champagne then all you're doing is collecting details of people who want to win a bottle of champagne rather than, for example, 12 hours of Accountancy services.

I can see why people who perceive their businesses to be particularly un-sexy try to give away more exciting gifts, but it won't help you in the long run. OK, so if you give away 12 hours worth of accountancy services you're probably going to pick up less leads than with a bottle of champagne, but the important thing is that those leads will be qualified leads. They'll be people who are interested in finding an accountant.

GIVE AWAY AN IRRESISTIBLY LARGE AND RELEVANT PRIZE

When you're creating your competition, make your prize irresistibly large. As large as you can afford. And be specific. Don't just give people a free website. Make it a free website worth £1450. It's much, much more irresistible.

Here are some ideas to get you thinking.

BUSINESS	PRIZE
Accountancy Firm	Two months free accountancy services worth over £2000
Interior Designer	A free room scheme worth £850
Hotel at a small business exhibition	A meeting room to hold your first workshop, seminar or networking event in, including tea, coffee and bacon rolls for your guests worth £600.
Wedding photographer	Win a free shoot and luxury album of your wedding day – worth over £3000!
Tax advisor	Your tax return for the year – done! Just leave your name and contact details to be in with a chance.

Let's take the wedding photographer example. If you were at a wedding fair and you had already booked your photographer would you enter the competition? It's unlikely because you'd have put down a deposit for your day, so you'd spend your time looking at the other stands. By offering a prize that's relevant to your business you're sifting through the people who won't be interested, and you can spend your time with visitors who have more potential.

Of course this isn't completely foolproof. You'll find that a small proportion of people will enter the competition because they like the idea of winning something, even though their photographer is sorted out, but in the main it's a plan worth following.

CREATE A POSTER AND HAVE SOMETHING TO HOLD YOUR LEADS IN.

I use a clear glass vase, which always works well, but you could use a box, a tin or something more creative. A jar or other container full of business cards always draws a bit of passing interest, so make sure it's clearly visible.

And make sure you prop a small A4 or A5 poster up behind the container so that even if you're all busy chatting to prospective clients, other visitors can see what they need to do to win your fabulous prize.

MAKE NOTES ON THE BACK OF BUSINESS CARDS

You don't need to have just had a baby to suffer from acute short-term memory loss. Exhibitions are busy, you will have a lot of conversations and it's highly likely you will forget the details if you don't make notes. I guarantee you'll be thankful you have something to jog your memory in the morning.

PREPARE 'ENTRY FORMS' FOR THE PEOPLE THAT DON'T HAVE BUSINESS CARDS

At a business-to-business show you'll usually find that 80-90% of people carry business cards with them. But at a business-to-consumer show it'll be more like 10-20%. You need to find another way of capturing data from your leads.

Many exhibition trainers advocate clipboards, but I'm not a fan of this concept. I think they work well to record requests for more information on, but they're not going to work for a prize draw. You need to demonstrate to people that you're going to pick one name, and to do that you need entry forms.

Make sure you get the key contact details: name, email address, telephone number, address; also gather anything else that will help you or that's relevant. For example, wedding date, how many employees they have or whether they have used a garden designer or not; whatever's relevant to your business.

Keep the entry forms as short as possible – the less people have to fill out, the more information they will give you. You don't want them to give up halfway through!

Ask people on the entry form if they'd like to be added to your mailing list to receive special offers, news and updates.

DATA PROTECTION

I do not profess to be an expert in this area, but this is what the Business Link website says on the matter:

You should tell individuals what you will use their personal information for, and make sure that your use of personal information does not break any other laws. When you obtain personal information, you must tell individuals:

- *The name of your business or organization*
- *What you use their information for*
- *Any other information needed to make your use of their personal information fair*

Generally, you cannot pass individuals' information to another business or organisation unless you have asked for - and they have given - their consent.

For the definitive guide visit http://www.ico.gov.uk/

It's probably unlikely that you'll want to pass data to another company, I certainly wouldn't advocate it. What's key is that when you start communicating with people you explain why they are on your mailing list, and you give them the opportunity to opt out.

Bear in mind that the rules seem to be much stricter for marketing to individuals than to businesses.

HAVE A SYSTEM IN PLACE TO MANAGE YOUR LEADS.

You'll need to think about how you're going to manage all these leads. Do you already have a database in place?

At the very least put them onto something like an Excel spreadsheet or your Outlook contacts. Better still, use one of the very low cost database systems that are available online. What's key is that you keep your contacts in a format that you can use for mail merges and emails and also for making a note of your telephone conversations.

WRITE A COMMUNICATION PLAN TO CONTACT PEOPLE AFTER THE SHOW VIA EMAIL, POST AND TELEPHONE

We've talked above about following up via telephone, email and post. Before your exhibition, plan what you will do with your leads once it is over; that way you commit to making things happen and your good intentions don't go out the window!

SCHEDULE IN TIME FOR THE FOLLOW-UP

Once you've got this bundle of leads, make life easy for yourself by putting aside time for your telephone follow-up. And don't forget to factor in time to put these leads onto your database and to stuff envelopes. The last thing you want is to be so drawn into your day-to-day activities that you put aside your leads and forget about them. Of course you're likely to win a bit of business, but you will significantly increase the business you win if you follow-up effectively.

CHECKLIST

- ❐ Run a competition
- ❐ Create marketing literature for before, during and after the event
- ❐ Have a system in place to manage your leads.
- ❐ Prepare 'entry forms'
- ❐ Create a poster and have something to hold your leads in.

PART THREE: AT THE EXHIBITION

The big day is finally here. All that hard work you've put in is about to pay off. You're about to build relationships with people, gain hundreds (hopefully) of good leads for your business and raise the profile of your company. How can you make the most of the day?

In this chapter we'll look at the finishing touches for your stand, how best to handle your enquiries and how you make sure you present your very best self on the day.

Let's start with your stand.

BUILDING AND DRESSING YOUR STAND

Rule number one of building a great stand is to do it in advance. Don't be one of those exhibitors who gets there in the morning, five minutes before the show opens, and races to get their stand together. Exhibitions are all about you presenting the very best of your business to visitors: you wrestling with a roll of Velcro and your pop-up stand is not a good look.

Allow plenty of time to get to the event and make sure you do the set-up the night before the show. I always find that I forget something, and if I leave set-up until the day it leaves me with very little opportunity to replace what I've forgotten.

Make a list, cross check it and check it again to make sure you haven't forgotten anything. Here's a small list for the stand build; you'll find a full list of things you might need to take to an exhibition at the back of this book.

BUILDING YOUR STAND CHECKLIST

- ❒ Posters
- ❒ Pop up/ pull up stand
- ❒ Furniture
- ❒ Velcro to stick posters directly to the shell scheme
- ❒ Container to put your leads in

STAND PERSONNEL

In the hubbub of creating posters, ordering your name badges, writing your piece for the showguide and getting on with your everyday work, it's easy to forget about briefing your stand staff. But finding, training and briefing the right staff for your business is essential.

TIME & RESOURCE MANAGEMENT

Successful exhibitors always make sure they have enough, but not an overwhelming amount, of staff on their stand. It's a tough balancing act between making sure you have enough resources at the show and keeping the office going too. If you're exhibiting at a local show, managing your resources becomes a whole lot easier because you can just draft people in as and when you need them.

How many people you have on your stand will depend on how you intend to manage your enquiries on the day, which we'll come on to shortly. You also need to make sure that you don't overwhelm visitors with too many of your own staff, which could put off browsers. At local exhibitions with up to 1,000 visitors I usually have two members of staff on the stand all day, and I draft in an extra pair of hands to help out with the 10am-2pm slot which is generally the busiest. I recommend you use your experience or ask the organisers of your show what they suggest.

You'll need to account for tea and coffee breaks, and lunch breaks, which I confess never happen for me at exhibitions! I always make sure my staff have breaks, but they tend to happen after 2pm when things get a little quieter.

You'll need to brief your team fully on what you want to achieve from the day, and it's worth getting together to brainstorm your approach as well as delegating specific tasks.

SELECT STAFF WHO ARE KNOWLEDGEABLE, ENTHUSIASTIC AND CAN SELL THE BUSINESS VERY WELL.

Because exhibitions are all about bringing your company to life, selecting, briefing and training your stand staff is absolutely essential. You need to make sure that not only do they look the part, but also that they know their stuff and reflect your brand positively.

Think about what makes your business unique. Do you pride yourself on your friendly, bubbly approach? Is it your professional, no-nonsense detailed approach that people come to you for? Whatever makes you unique, make sure the people you put on your stand reflect those values. They have got to know your product or service inside out, they've got to be enthusiastic and they must be able to sell your business well.

GET YOUR STAFF INVOLVED EARLY ON IN THE PLANNING

You never know, they might just have some good ideas! Getting staff involved from the outset ensures that they are as enthusiastic as you are about the event and that they will help you get the best return on your investment. So include them in your planning meetings, discuss your layout ideas with them and show them the artwork – get their feedback. Better to hear it from them than your potential clients!

MAKE SURE THEY UNDERSTAND THE OBJECTIVES OF THE SHOW

You want them to take 30 bookings for branding consultations? Tell them! They're more likely to get there if they have goals.

You want them to gain 100 leads by 2pm? Again, tell them (and give them a prize when they do). Just a quick word of warning on that one. I always have to physically restrain myself from counting my leads! It's soooo tempting: watching that vase fill up with business cards and just knowing that there's plenty of potential business in there. But you must resist. I think it must look terrible to any passers-by if people sit there counting their leads.

ENSURE THEY HAVE SUFFICIENT PRODUCT KNOWLEDGE (IN TIME!).

Are you launching a new product? Give your staff at least a couple of weeks to gen up on the product. Give them a crib sheet to go away and learn. And test them! School-marmish? Maybe, but you don't want them looking useless on the day, so give yourselves plenty of time to prepare in advance.

Better still, role play and provide your team with a crib sheet for any frequently asked questions.

INCENTIVISE THEM – SET UP A COMPETITION TO SEE WHO CAN GAIN THE MOST LEADS!

Competitive staff? Set up a competition to reward the person who goes the furthest to meeting your objectives – whether that's booking events, selling subscriptions or gaining leads. Whatever your objectives, if you can measure it, reward it!

BRIEF THEM THOROUGHLY ON YOUR BRAND IMAGE

How do you want potential customers and existing customers to perceive you? This should run through everything, from the design of your stand to the way you and your staff are dressed and your tone of voice.

BRING PLENTY OF WATER AND QUICKLY-EATABLE SWEETS FOR THEM

If it's a good show then you will be run off your feet and you probably won't have time for a break. At least not till after 2/3pm when it gets much quieter. So take sweets that can be eaten quickly and surreptitiously just off the stand.

TAKE THEM OUT FOR DINNER TO SAY THANK YOU

It's been a long couple of days and you're all exhausted. But if you've had a good show and you all feel up to it why not take your staff (and your partner) out for dinner to say thank you, and celebrate a little. We always feel pretty jubilant at the end of a show and it's nice to share your success with the people that have helped you get there.

CREATING THE RIGHT IMPRESSION

Here's some more tips to help you get the best out of the day.

- Make sure there's always someone on your stand. This won't be possible if there's only one of you, so draft in some help.

- Be approachable: Smile and look welcoming! Look as if you're happy to be there and people will want to talk to you.

- Pack mints and water for the stand. Even those of us with the freshest of breath can find that a whole day talking can leave us feeling rather stale. Take a slurp of water whenever you can. And as for mints, make sure you can eat them quickly and discreetly.

- Don't eat smelly food. Look, I love tuna and garlic and spring onions (not necessarily together) as much as the next person, but an exhibition is not the place to eat them! So when you leave your stand to fuel-up, stick to food that's not going to leave a nasty taste or smell in your mouth on your return.

- Don't eat on your stand. OK, I know I've told you to eat mints, but that's really it. No one is going to visit your stand if you're chowing down on a huge sub roll with mayo dripping down your shirt.

- Make sure you're well groomed – fingernails, hair, teeth! Pack a hairbrush, toothbrush and toothpaste for a quick perk up halfway through the day.

- Wear plenty of (subtle) make-up (ladies only!) You want to look your best, so make sure your make-up looks good. You'll need it to look natural but presentable. Take a top-up of perhaps lipstick and blusher for partway through the day: it can get hot on those stands, especially if you have a lot of lights.

- Guys can benefit from mosturiser, exfoliating to get rid of any peeling skin, and a little blusher if you're so inclined (and naturally pale!).

- If you are socialising the night before, drink moderately. Exhibitions often give companies a chance to come together and bond, but alcohol sweats are so not a good look for your stand, so take it easy on the wine. Those bright lights make a hangover worse and you won't be able to focus properly. Trust me, I speak from experience.

HANDLING ENQUIRIES

When I worked as a Regional Director for a large chain of print franchises, twice a year we would take a stand at the London and Birmingham Franchise Shows. It was always an exciting (and exhausting) couple of days. The marketing team would put together a fantastic stand and staff from all around the country would gather together to promote our franchise opportunity.

We would take an enormous area and have live talks, videos and demonstrations with designers creating business cards live on Macs for the delegates. Every year we would walk away with a huge amount of leads, which in turn translated into franchisee sales.

But how did we get the balance right between focusing on building our database and spending quality time with hot sales leads?

One of the biggest challenges in selling a franchise is communicating effectively with your market. Generally the types of people who buy a franchise are senior managers, often in sales and marketing roles. How do you talk to them? Well you could place ads and editorial in the management magazines. But then a large proportion of those people aren't going to be in the market for buying a franchise. The next best step is to use the franchise press. But you still lack a two-way conversation with these people. And you miss the opportunity to mail to them directly.

By far and away the best way of finding out who is interested in buying a franchise is to exhibit at the franchise shows. You're gaining access here to a group of people who are actively looking at whether becoming a franchise is right for them. Here's a fantastic opportunity to build a database of people who are looking to invest in a franchise.

Not only did we qualify these leads, we understood where people were at in the process. Some people had read up on us, looked at the proposal and had come to the show with the express intention of taking the franchise opportunity further. So we needed an area to sit and chat to these people. And we identified key members of staff who would handle this process. The most senior members of staff – the Chief Executive, the Franchise Director and the Operations Director handled these conversations.

Then there was a group of people who were interested in buying a print franchise and were checking out all the options. These were usually dealt with by the Regional Directors and we would agree to follow-up with a more senior manager after the show. Importantly, we were streamlining our prospects to make the best use of our time at the event.

Next, there were the people who hadn't had exposure to printing.com until the exhibition, but who liked what they saw. Their details were recorded and they were followed up afterwards.

And finally, there were the people who we spoke to who had no intention of investing in a printing.com franchise: perhaps they were competitors, or their investment capital was too low, or they were simply looking for a different opportunity. So the junior members of the stand staff would often qualify these people and sort the hot from the, shall we say, cooler, prospects! Would you spend time with these people? As little as possible ideally! Would you capture their data? Probably not, to be honest. Better to spend time connecting with your warmer leads.

Whoever we spoke to, however hot or cold, it was important to maintain a friendly, professional and warm manner so that they got a positive impression of the company.

MANAGING YOUR ENQUIRIES

Think back to your show objectives. Are you going to sell, build your database, or do you have more strategic aims? You'll probably want to split your team up so that your top salespeople deal with your hottest prospects, and the more junior members manage the general enquiries.

The model that's always worked for me is:

1. Capture as many targeted leads for my database on the day as possible

2. Qualify leads and spend time with the hottest prospects on the stand, booking a meeting after the event if possible

3. Categorise leads immediately (ie. Evening after) the event

4. Follow-up immediately

5. Convert as many into clients as possible after the event

Ideally you'll have plenty of stand staff so that you manage to speak to everyone interested.

QUALIFY YOUR LEADS AND FILTER YOUR BEST PEOPLE TO SPEAK TO THE HOTTEST LEADS

Try and have more staff than you need if possible – you can always send them home (if it's a local show of course!). If the business is just you, then don't forget that you can always rope in friends and family. Make sure they're well briefed on your aims for the show and also your brand and they will be a great asset to you.

Ideally you'll streamline your enquiries so that your best salespeople are dealing with the hot, well-qualified leads and your most junior members of staff are working on the more run-of-the-mill enquiries, perhaps qualifying them or selling the smaller-value products.

Whatever you do, gather as much information as you can and make sure you send them away with some compelling marketing literature.

There's nothing more frustrating than being stuck with someone who is trying to sell you something, and seeing what could be hot prospects, or perhaps great clients, in the background.

DON'T TRY AND SELL TO OTHER EXHIBITORS WHILE THEY'RE BUSY!

And while we're on the subject of people trying to sell you things on the stand, can I just share a moment of etiquette here? Please, please, please refrain from trying to sell to other exhibitors on their stand. Whether you're at the show as an exhibitor or a visitor, nothing is more infuriating than having someone monopolise your time and try and sell to you.

As exhibitors we're all here to sell, and if you've spotted someone you'd like to make contact with, why not wait until the exhibition dies down – usually after 2pm, especially while the seminars are going on. That's a bit more acceptable, but don't butt in while someone has a busy stand, you're just not being fair.

WHAT IF I GET STUCK WITH SOMEONE TRYING TO SELL TO ME?

That's tricky. Whilst the temptation is to say "Look, I've spent a lot of money on this stand and I'm here to win business. Now please go away and let me get on with it." From experience, I'd suggest that's not the best way to handle it! Instead I recommend you interrupt their usually torrential flow with their name and politely tell them that it sounds interesting and could you give them your card so that you can make contact after the exhibition.

SELLING ON THE STAND

If you have a product in the £10-50 range then you'll often be able to sell your products on the day. Generally, the higher the price tag, the longer the sales cycle, so you'll probably sell £50-£150 products pretty quickly after the show.

One of the reasons I converted so many of my clients after my first show was because I had a low entry point product: many of them bought business cards for £49 which made it a very low-commitment way of testing us out.

Products in excess of £150 are much harder, although not impossible, to sell on your stand. Here's how you can get the most out of selling on your stand.

USE PROMOTIONS TO GENERATE INSTANT BUSINESS

If you are looking to generate immediate sales at an exhibition then you must offer some kind of special deal or discount. There is something in the psyche of a visitor at an exhibition that compels them to buy if there's a deal in it for them. Fail to offer a discount for orders placed on the day and people will simply go away and 'think about it'. Which is code for forget about it. Of course you will get people ordering, but not in the volumes that they would if you offered them a too-good-to-miss deal for orders placed on the day.

OFFER A DISCOUNT FOR ORDERS PLACED ON THE DAY

Visitors don't just want a deal, they expect a deal. And the better the deal, the more sales you'll make. Personally my feeling is that it's got to be a good deal. And 10% or less doesn't count as a good deal.

Does 10% tip you over the edge if you're considering buying? Not usually. If you were going to buy anyway then great, you get a discount, but if you were wavering it's probably not quite enough. So all that you end up with as a business is giving away 10% of your profits to people who were going to buy anyway.

If you're going to discount, then give something decent – 15% up to 50% is ideal. And make sure you say it's for orders placed today only.

CONSIDER EXTENDING A SMALLER DISCOUNT OVER A PERIOD OF TIME

Let's say you were offering 25% off orders placed today. Why not offer 15% on orders placed within the two weeks immediately following the show? I wouldn't promote that on the day of the exhibition; I'd have it on my takeaway promotional literature, my exhibition web page and also ready in my follow-up email. The real benefit of this is that you capture another wave of people who were wavering at the show, and hopefully this will just tip them over the edge.

DON'T WANT TO OFFER A DISCOUNT? HOW ABOUT A BOGOF OR SPECIAL DEAL?

Some businesses are uncomfortable about offering a discount. That might be because they don't feel it fits with their brand image. It could be because your business model doesn't have the scope for a discount. A wine merchant client of mine makes such a low margin that they simply can't afford to give away more than 10%, which let's face it, is pretty uninviting. But offering a mini bottle of champagne with all case orders over £100? Now that's more enticing!

So if you don't want to offer a discount, how about a Buy One Get One Free (BOGOF) offer? Or a gift when you buy x. You could offer an eBook, a workshop, earrings when you buy the necklace and bracelet... Whatever you think will compel people to buy right now.

THINK ABOUT GIVING A SMALLER GIFT WITH ORDERS PLACED WITHIN 2 WEEKS OR SO OF YOUR EVENT

Just as with the discount, if you're offering a gift instead of a discount offer a smaller one for people who order within a couple of weeks, or whatever you think is an appropriate time frame. But do make sure it's a smaller gift. You don't want to annoy the people who bought on the day to get your special deal by offering the same deal in a couple of weeks. It just makes you look bad.

HAVE PROMOTIONAL MATERIAL WITH YOUR DISCOUNTS/ COMPETITION ON YOUR STAND FOR PEOPLE YOU DON'T MANAGE TO TALK TO

You're not going to be able to talk to every single visitor, or even every single interested visitor, at most exhibitions. If your stand is impressive enough, your offering well tailored and your competition and live demonstration powerful enough, chances are you'll be too busy to talk to everyone. So you need to create some promotional literature advertising your discounts that people can take away and use to order online after the event.

Use a special discount code so that you can track the success of the event, and make sure the offer is nice and prominent.

CREATE A LOW COST PRODUCT THAT GIVES PEOPLE A TASTER OF WHAT YOU DO

If you sell a 'high ticket' item that costs say, more than £500, why not create a product that's much cheaper and gives people the opportunity to 'taste' what you do. That might be a short consultation session, a book, a workshop or a much smaller physical product. Be creative, brainstorm with friends and colleagues and see what you can come up with.

So you've had a great day, gathered hundreds of leads and made some great contacts. Your work has just begun! Let's look at how you can make the most of your leads in the next section.

AT THE EXHIBITION CHECKLIST

- ☐ Choose the right stand staff, Incentivise them and brief them thoroughly
- ☐ Plan how you'll manage your enquiries
- ☐ Put a plan in place to boost your sales on the day
- ☐ Pick up more sales after the event too, by extending your offer

PART FOUR: AFTER THE EXHIBITION

People often ask me what one thing they can do to improve their success at exhibitions, and I always tell them that the key is in the follow-up (assuming you have enough leads to start with of course). If there's one area many exhibitors catastrophically miss opportunities, it's in the (lack of) follow-up.

The single most important thing that you can do after an event is to follow-up quickly and persistently. The second most important thing is to have a marketing plan in place to be able to maintain contact for the next few years.

In this sector we're going to look at cost-effective ways of following-up after an exhibition, and also how to do the all-important review to see how successful the event was for you.

FOLLOW-UP

If you want to convert a high proportion of leads into paying customers then you must follow-up systematically and promptly. Remember, if you don't follow-up quickly enough, you can be sure that your competitors will!

You need to make sure you:

- Make contact within a maximum of 48 hours after the event – the simplest way to do this is via email

- Send out more information to those who have asked for it within 3 working days

- Start the telephone follow-ups to your hottest leads the next working day, and aim to have completed all telephone calls within 2 weeks

Now you're not going to be able to do any of that if you get back from your event and then need to start writing emails, telephone scripts and sales letters. You've got to get organised and get all of this prepared before your exhibition.

I'd recommend you prepare:

- An email immediately after the event
- A second email a week later
- A covering letter to send to people who have requested 'more information'
- 'More information' – does that mean a lovely glossy brochure?
- A telephone script so that your team and perhaps a telemarketing agency can follow-up
- An autoresponder sequence that you can use to deliver short chunks of information simply (see below).

HOW DID I CONVERT 70% OF MY LEADS INTO PAYING CUSTOMERS?

Do you remember my story of the exhibition that kick-started my business back in 2005? When I tell people I converted 70% of my initial exhibition leads into customers they're always shocked. They're usually surprised that I converted such a high percentage of leads because that's not the experience they usually have. But I'm not telling you this to gloat, I'm sharing this story with you because there's an important point here. I converted so many of my leads into paying customers because I kept in touch with them.

I kept in touch with my leads every month, at least once a month, by email, telephone or mail.

I called every single contact until I got through to them. Most people would attempt to call once or twice and then give up. I made sure I called every single person until I got through to them. The exhibition was in June, and by the end of August I was still calling the odd straggler that I hadn't managed to get hold of.

I told them that they'd left their details with me at Winning Business yesterday/ last week/ last month and I wondered if there was anything in particular they were interested in.

I told them that I'd just started a design and print business in Guildford and that **I'd love to help them.** People responded especially well to this because we all like to support and encourage a new business (not that I'm suggesting you lie if you're not a new business!). I asked them if I could send them some samples or any quotes.

I asked them how they found the show and if they had gained anything from it. And **I asked them about their businesses:** what they did, who their clients were and how they marketed themselves. I gave them ideas and suggestions as to how they might market their businesses and I built relationships with them.

Over the years I've learnt that there is no more powerful way of building a relationship with a client or potential client than to ask them about themselves... and listen to the response! We all love to talk about ourselves and even the frostiest, most impatient person will melt when you spend time talking to them about their business, their children or their animals.

I suspect that if I had measured how much business we'd won by the end of August, the answer would be very little. But within a year that figure was substantially higher: you've got to be patient, and persistent!

IMMEDIATELY AFTER THE EXHIBITION: PRIORITISE YOUR LEADS

I usually do this the evening of the show. Once I've drawn my prizewinner I'll usually count up the leads (well, I've resisted all day!) and then sort them into three envelopes:

- Follow-up immediately – 24-48 hours after the event
- Follow-up within a week
- No immediate need, make telephone contact within 2-3 weeks

✐ Prioritising your leads

You'll probably have a strong sense of who needs following up first in order to maximise the initial sales from the event, but here's some guidance in case you're new to this.

Start by reading the notes on the back of the cards. For the cards that don't have any notes on them and look at the company names to see if you recognise any as clients (or competitors!).

I sort the cards into three piles that I then place in envelopes and take to the office the next day to start the telephone calls.

☐ **Pile One: Follow-up immediately.** These will usually be people who have expressed a desire to book a meeting or buy something from you immediately.

☐ **Pile Two: Follow-up within a week.** You think there is a lot of potential to do business with these people but they have no imminent need for anything. Alternatively, they may be people you didn't speak to on the day, so you don't know what the potential is. You need to call them quickly and find out!

☐ **Pile Three: Make telephone contact within 2-3 weeks.** They're unlikely to want to do business with you in the near future, or they may be a competitor! It's still very worthwhile taking the time to follow up on these things. You never know where your conversations might take you.

PUT THEM ON YOUR DATABASE

As quickly as I possibly can I also enter these leads onto a database, usually within 1-2 days, so that I can get an email out to them. If you don't have a database then you'll find some ideas in the Useful Contacts section at the back of this book.

If you know you're unlikely to have the time to enter dozens of enquiries on to your database as well as following-up with phone calls then arrange for a temp or college student to come in for the two days after the exhibition so that they can be putting enquiries on the database while you follow-up.

When you enter your leads onto your database don't forget to organise by source so that you know where you found these leads. If you can, also make sure that you put some notes in to remind you of any conversations you had with them.

COLLATERAL TO FOLLOW UP WITH AFTER THE EVENT.

We've discussed the importance of following up effectively in previous chapters, and I've outlined here some of the collateral you'll need to think about creating alongside some suggested approaches. Of course, you'll probably find that you're already doing much of these, and if they work, then don't feel that you must change them. I just outline here what works for me.

THE FOLLOW-UP EMAIL

Your follow-up email will ideally be sent out within 24 hours of your exhibition, or 48 hours if you have hundreds of leads! Obviously what you write will depend on your natural writing style, your products and services, and the aims of your exhibition. Here are a few pointers to help you. You'll probably want to include:

- Why they're getting this email (because we met at the X Show yesterday and you entered our competition to win...)
- To let them know how often you'll keep in touch and that they can unsubscribe at any time
- Who won the competition and their reaction
- Not to worry if you didn't win, here's a special offer for people we met at the X Show yesterday, valid for x days
- A very short paragraph about your business, perhaps referring them to your website to find out more

You'll find an example of one of our follow up emails in the Appendices at the back of this book.

A REMINDER EMAIL

You'll probably want to send this email out within 5-10 days of your first email, depending on the offer you have made your new contacts. The goal of this email is to remind them about you and your company and also to prompt them to use your special offer. This one is probably much more simple and will probably include:

- A reminder to use your special discount before x
- Progress/ case study on your competition winner if relevant/ appropriate
- An invitation to book for a consultation/ tasting/ visit your website/ download information if relevant

A COVERING LETTER

Your covering letter will accompany whatever your 'more information' is (more information on that below...). Resist the temptation to send out your normal covering letter. Create a bespoke letter that explains to your potential client why they would be interested in your product or service. Outline one of the key benefits that you think visitors of that exhibition would find particularly attractive. Make a time-bound exclusive offer if you can, and include a testimonial. And try and keep it to no more than a page.

'MORE INFORMATION'

What do you send people when they ask for more information? The same old leaflet you gave them at the show? A link to your website? If you do then you're missing a trick. People have asked for 'more information' because they're interested but they need a bit more persuading that they should buy from you. If they already have your leaflet, how is sending them the same old thing going to impress them?

A lovely, glossy brochure is what most people think of when they ask for more information. We also send people samples and invite them to come and have a chat and look at our portfolio. Many textile and wallpaper companies will send samples or paint charts, and sometimes a brochure which shows how these work in context.

If you really, really don't have the budget for a brochure, how about creating a PDF brochure that you can email? Make it really well designed, with powerful copy and you're still giving your audience that 'more information' that they crave.

Also think about having case studies and testimonials ready to email at the drop of a hat. Find a great branding and design company (I've heard printing.com in Guildford are very good...) to create a design for you that will work across all your marketing to make you look more cohesive and professional.

A TELEPHONE SCRIPT

If the idea of having a telephone script fills you with horror, then let's reframe it. Think of your telephone script as the chance for you, and anyone else in your business who makes follow-up calls, to brainstorm what you want to get out of the call and how you're going to manage it.

I'm not suggesting for one moment that you script this word for word, but just take the opportunity to think in advance about how you'd like the calls to work and anything that you think is essential to communicate.

You may like to think about:

- The purpose of the call – why will you tell the contact you're calling?
- Goal of the call – what do you want to get out of the call? A sale? A meeting an event or workshop booking? Permission to mail some information?
- Do you need to gain more information from the client?
- Do you need to give out any more information?

AN AUTORESPONDER

Autoresponders are marvellous tools. They enable you to send out emails over a pre-determined period of time, so you might use them to send out your 10 tips, or information after you've sold a product. The best thing about them is that you can send information out to multiple people in a specific order, and no matter when you put these contacts on your database, you'll always keep the emails going out in the right order and the right distance apart.

I'm aware this seems like a lot of work, but this exhibition isn't the cheapest marketing activity you're going to do this year. Do it well, and it will pay off, but preparing your marketing collateral is an area where you shouldn't be cutting corners. Start planning early and you'll find that you enter this exhibition with a sense of calm and success before you've even started!

THE LONG-TERM FOLLOW-UP

If one of the major benefits of an exhibition is the influx of quality leads you'll add to your database, then you need to have a plan for keeping in touch with these leads, and that's what we'll look at now.

KEEPING IN TOUCH.

While most business owners appreciate that they need to follow-up on the leads gained at an exhibition, many fail to keep in touch on an ongoing basis.

For many buyers, the purchasing cycle can be a long one: often months, or even years. Let's take someone visiting the Grand Designs Live show for example. Are they ready to buy immediately? Or have they gone with the intention of gaining some ideas this year, perhaps having some plans drawn up and maybe putting in planning permission next year.

If you sell taps then it's going to be a long time before that visitor is ready to buy from you. But it doesn't mean that they won't! And this is where a lot of people fall down when it comes to keeping in touch with their leads.

So as well as planning the collateral you'll need for the day, I think it's essential that you put in place a communications strategy to help maximise your brand exposure and win more business over several years, not just in the months following the exhibition.

EMAIL NEWSLETTERS

Once you've thoroughly followed-up with your contacts on the immediate opportunities you'll want to integrate them into your normal promotional cycle. This means keeping them up-to-date with news, special offers, product launches and helpful information, like newsletters on a regular basis. And you really need to be keeping in passive contact like this on a fortnightly to monthly basis via email.

"Email my database once a month?" Yes! Absolutely. One of the great benefits of email is that it's instant. The biggest downside is that it's also instantly forgotten. You must keep in touch with people on a very regular basis, every 2-4 weeks or you risk being forgotten about. And if your clients forget about you, you can bet that one of your more marketing-savvy competitors is going to keep plugging away with the marketing and guess who that contact is going to go to when they need your product or service? Chances are it won't be you because you'll be long forgotten.

I email my contacts around 4 times a month. Does it annoy them? Some, probably. Every email I send out (and I send out to almost 2,000 contacts) I will get a couple of 'unsubscribes'. But do you know, for every 'unsubscribe', I get twice as many positive bits of feedback. And it's a rare moment that people forget about me or my business – I don't let them!

If you think "I'll start a newsletter once a quarter", forget it. Just don't waste your time. Newsletters, special offers, blogs – they've got to be regular to work for you.

SEND OUT REGULAR MAILINGS

As well as email, make sure you mail-out regularly too. I send a mail-out every month to about 400 contacts with my special offer of the month.

And I also mail at certain times of the year with other information. OK, so mailing costs more and takes longer, but the impact is so much greater.

Many of us receive over 100 emails a day and we get information overload. One message merges into the next into the next and we delete all but the most important in a fit of pique. Email might be free, it might be quick, but it's not enough to get your message through on its' own. And so you've got to find new ways, more powerful ways of getting your message across. What's key is that you mix up your marketing. Don't just stick to mailing or emailing, but combine the two with networking and sales calls to get a balanced and effective marketing message across.

A LONG TERM COMMUNICATION PLAN

When you're planning your marketing activities you'll need to create a balanced mix. Try to include some 'direct response' offers via email, mail and the internet, alongside some softer 'branding'/ value-adding newsletters, blogs and articles to raise your profile and build relationships. You'll also want to think about live events such as workshops to bring your business to life, as well as online and offline networking.

However you choose to market your business, keep in mind that you must build relationships with your clients, keep yourself front of mind, and entice your leads to buy from you.

I'm not going to go into lots of detail about marketing planning because that could fill an entire book! But here's some suggested ways of keeping in touch and building a relationship with your database (you don't need to do them all!).

- Email newsletter
- Email offers
- Telephone calls
- Regular mailings of monthly offers
- Blogging and Social networking: Twitter, LinkedIn, Facebook etc

REVIEW

So how did it all go? Did your hard work pay off? Your gut feel is a useful tool, so don't dismiss it, but it's also helpful to do some hard analysis. Let's take your SMART goals and analyse them against your results.

MEASURING AGAINST YOUR SMART GOALS

Remember those goals we created way back before the exhibition? Time to pull them out and see if you achieved what you set out to.

Some will be very easy to measure. Did you pick up the target number of leads you set out to? Did you manage to distribute as much collateral as you'd hoped? Measuring your target number of clients might be a little harder depending on when you review this.

I recommend you review immediately after the show, after one month, after three months, six months and twelve months. If you keep this as a separate spreadsheet then you'll have a good record for next time you exhibit.

Take a look also at how much the average show client spends compared to your average client. Take a look at the section below on KPI's for how to do that.

KEY PERFORMANCE INDICATORS

When I worked in for a big company, logging and reviewing Key Performance Indicators (KPI's) with my Store Managers was a key part of our regular tasks. Every month we'd review them to understand how and why the company was performing as it was, and use that information to plan for the next month.

There are lots of things that I have been very glad to leave behind in the corporate world, but KPI's are one of the things that I've retained over the past four years, and I use them to guide me through the highs and lows of my business.

They're so useful that I passionately believe every business should be using them. And yet how many people know what they are? Let alone what to do with them! Here's my introduction to Key Performance Indicators (KPI's) and why you should be using them in your business.

HELPING YOU MEASURE WHAT MAKES YOUR BUSINESS SUCCESSFUL.

Key Performance Indicators, as the name suggests, are the key indicators of success in your business. Now they'll vary from business to business, but here are some of the things that I measure on a monthly basis:

- ☐ Turnover
- ☐ Gross Profit
- ☐ GP as a %
- ☐ Number of Customers
- ☐ Number of Orders
- ☐ Average Order Value
- ☐ Average Customer Spend
- ☐ Number of Enquiries
- ☐ Conversion Ratio from Enquiries to Customers.

What are the key things that make a difference in your business?
Perhaps it's the product mix? It might be the efficiency of production? You should also use them to measure the less great stuff- any complaints or quality issues that you can monitor on a monthly basis.

Now this sort of information is reasonably useful on a one-off basis but it really comes into it's own when you start tracking it over a longer period of time. Once you have six months or more to compare you can really start to see trends happening, and comparing year on year results helps you plan for the quiet times and manic cycles in your business.

I look at my KPI's to **understand why the business is performing as it is.** If we've had a particularly great month is that because we've attracted more customers? Had a higher spend from our customers? Sold more print jobs? Or converted a higher percentage of enquiries into customers? Without that information you're running blind. It's crucial that you (and your team) keep your finger on the pulse at all times so that you can act on the information and become even more successful.

✎ Recording your own KPIs

☐ Take a blank excel spreadsheet.

☐ Write each Key Performance Indicator down the side in column A.

☐ Write the months of the year along the top. Now it's simple, every month you record the relevant bits of information.

I try to do this by the first week of the new month so that I can act on the information (good and bad) quickly. I share my KPI's with my team, and together we interpret the results in our weekly meetings.

GAIN FEEDBACK

As well as hard facts, try to gain some subjective feedback about the exhibition and how well your stand was received. Talk to your colleagues, how well did they think you did? What could you do better in the future?

How about your clients that visited you at the show? What did they make of the exhibition itself? How about your stand? Use their feedback to improve what you do next time. Make a point of also asking your new contacts for their opinions; many people love to give their two-eggs worth, and in showing them you value their opinion you're also forging stronger relationships.

FORWARD PLANNING

Whether this was your first event or your fiftieth, the chances are that every time you exhibit you'll call upon previous experiences to make your next event even more successful.

It's easy to forget the highs and lows between exhibitions, so jot down a few notes, save any marketing collateral you've created, and file away your evaluation into a folder. You'll then be able to access it next time you do an exhibition, which will make everything so much more productive.

✐ Exhibition Notes

How many times do you find yourself scrambling around trying to find what you wrote for last year's showguide entry? Put together a folder full of useful notes for each exhibition. I like to include items such as:

❏ Number of leads gained

❏ Number of clients gained after one month, 3 months, 6 months and 12 months

❏ Competition winner and outcome

❏ Event successes

❏ Things to do better next time

❏ Feedback from clients and colleagues

THE LAST WORD

So here we are, at the end of the book. We've looked at how a little planning, focus and creativity will make a big difference to how successful your next exhibition is. We've discussed the importance of making a good impression with your stand and how you can follow-up for maximum impact.

I hope I've given you plenty of food for thought along the way, and that you'll be able to put into practice what you've learned to grow your business.

Do let me know how you get on. You can tweet me @fionahumberston or visit www.fionahumberstone.com for more ways to get in touch. I look forward to hearing from you.

CASE STUDIES AND RECOMMENDED APPROACHES.

If writing this book has taught me one thing, it's that there is no one-size-fits-all approach that will work for every business. Each market has it's own idiosyncrasies, tried and tested methods and tactics that simply won't work with a particular brand or client base.

What I hope is that you'll be able to pick up plenty of ideas that enable you to make your next exhibition more successful. And to help you do that I've put together some case studies that you can use to see how I might approach each project depending on the company.

"We had an extremely successful few days at the Designer Wedding Show in February, and the marketing advice that Fiona and Caroline gave me definitely contributed to this. We had a clear message at the show, and crucially are now implementing the follow-up strategy they came up with."
Clare Yarwood-White

YARWOOD-WHITE JEWELLERY

Clare Yarwood-White is Creative Director and owner of award-winning bridal jeweller Yarwood-White.com. Clare asked us to help her sell more products at the Designer Wedding show this year, so we worked with her to create an inspirational stand, plan some on-the-day discounts, and most importantly, create a communication plan to follow-up with after the show.

Clare's goal was to increase the number of orders she took at the show, and with our help, she doubled her sales this year! So how did she do it?

Yarwood-White have always had an impressive stand, so there was very little to do to help Clare build on that. They had just launched their "Modern Heirloom" collection which takes it's inspiration from the idea of mixing the old with the new: raiding Granny's jewellery box and blending her pearls with modern pieces. For the stand we wanted to carry this theme forward, so Clare sourced vintage cake stands, china cups, old mirrors and beautiful furniture to set the scene.

Clare had also arranged for a hairdresser to come and do some on-stand demonstrations, which pulled in a tremendous crowd! In fact, the stand was so busy that many visitors didn't manage to speak to the Yarwood-White team. Good job we had some leaflets around the edge of the stand then!

As an experienced exhibitor, Clare had also developed a great strategy for handling enquiries. Her team were proficient in weeding out those people who were unlikely to buy on the day, and giving them some information to take away. The 'hotter' leads were given the full Yarwood-White treatment : Clare herself, the Yarwood-White stylist or one of her team would spend time talking about the day each bride had planned, what the dress looked like, and how best to accessorise the look.

In the past, some brides had tended to go away and think about whether they wanted to buy the jewellery or not, but this year, **Yarwood-White offered an unprecedented 20% discount on all orders placed at the show. It was this discount that literally doubled their sales at the show.**

It's worth noting that the Yarwood-White team are not at all pushy sales people. That just wouldn't have worked. At the start of the show Clare briefed the team on their brand values: Assured, Alive and Available. Assured: confident as the market leaders in bridal jewellery. Alive: inspiring and enthusiastic when talking to brides about their plans for their wedding. Available: accessible and friendly and not at all stand-offish.

By reminding the stand staff of the company's brand values and how that translated through to being at the exhibition Clare could ensure that they were all projecting a consistent message to potential clients.

Most importantly, we worked with Clare to develop an after-show communication plan. Clare wrote a series of emails that could be mailed immediately to her new contacts, and one of those emails contained a 15% discount for all orders placed within the next two weeks.

IF YOU PLAN TO SELL PRODUCTS AT THE SHOW:

- ❐ Let people touch, feel and test your products

- ❐ Use evocative styling to bring your product to life

- ❐ Offer a discount for orders placed on the day

WEBLAUNCH, A SERVICE BUSINESS

Exhibitions are often much harder to make a success for a service-based or consultancy company because very often there's no 'product' for visitors to buy into. It makes sense to think about whether there are any products you can create from your range of services.

Bruce Hazleton and Ben Neale run The Marvellous Media Company which specialises in creating websites that attract visitors through the search engines and convert them into paying customers. Bruce and Ben sensibly diversified their business midway through this recession as the website market became saturated with top-end web design companies at roughly the same time as companies started slashing their website budgets.

This summer The Marvellous Media Company launched a very unique 'Pay As You Go' website concept called "WebLaunch" which enables customers to have a professionally designed website for just £25 a month.

WebLaunch was to be launched at three local business-to-business shows, and Bruce and I worked together to help them make their exhibitions a real success. The Marvellous Media Company were no strangers to exhibitions, but Bruce would probably be the first to admit that they hadn't especially capitalised on the potential of exhibitions in the past. Bruce was the client who admitted that he hadn't followed up on anything other than red-hot leads previously.

The first key area that made a difference for WebLaunch was to set themselves some targets. Bruce wanted to gain a very ambitious 25 new clients from each exhibition within three months. With no previous experience of what the conversion ratio would be (this project hadn't yet been launched) all we could do was plan, and keep our fingers crossed!

"Printing.com did a marvellous job on our WebLaunch branding and their advice on exhibiting was invaluable."

We worked on the basis of getting 50 leads and converting 50% of those into paying clients. And I'm pleased to say that two months on, those goals have been achieved!

Bruce and Ben branded their stand very well, with their WebLaunch frog taking pride of place not only on their stand, but on the staff's T-shirts too. Bruce had hoped to get one of the hotly contested website speaking slots, which had all been filled, so I suggested that he run short seminars off his stand.

It takes someone with guts to start a presentation with just a few passers-by, but by the end of each presentation Bruce had pulled in quite a crowd with his humorous and intelligent pitch.

Web Launch sold two websites at the show, with plenty of leads to follow-up on afterwards – 67 from the first show (of around 800 visitors) and 35 at the second show (which pulled in around 250 visitors).

The company's post-show communication was equally as quirky and impactful as their stand. Rather than sending round an email announcing the winner, WebLaunch made an occasion of drawing the winner. They asked someone to draw the names out of a sealed bag, video recorded it and posted it on YouTube. They then sent round an email inviting people to watch the video to see who had won.

CHECKLIST FOR SERVICE-BASED BUSINESSES:

- ☐ Create a low-cost 'product' that people can buy as a taster of your services

- ☐ Demonstrate your expertise

- ☐ Run a competition to capture data

THE HR DEPT, A CONSULTANCY

Consultancies face similar challenges to service-based companies, in that they don't usually have a 'product' for people to buy. It also usually takes a bit of imagination to create an impressive exhibition stand if you're a consultancy; most importantly, you need to design a product that can be closed at or just after an exhibition.

Ruth Sangale runs the HR Dept in Guildford which is an HR consultancy franchise. Ruth was exhibiting for the first time at a business-to-business show and was keen to get the most out of the event.

During her exhibit! Session we talked about Ruth's aims. She wanted visitors to know that HR is an essential service during a recession; to retain, motivate and manage redundancies. She wanted them to think that the HR Dept are really nice people who know their stuff, and she wanted them to enter a competition to win an HR manual, or buy a copy.

We brainstormed ways that she could bring her business to life and build relationships with people. We decided that one of the best things Ruth could do would be to offer five-minute consultancy sessions on any burning HR question, as well as top tips on getting the best out of your team.

Ruth had some low-cost HR workshops to sell after the exhibition so that gave her something very accessible to sell to people shortly after the event.

CHECKLIST FOR CONSULTANCIES:

- ❏ Create a 'product' that people can buy at or just after the show

- ❏ Build a database of people you can build a relationship with after the exhibition

- ❏ Give away free tips or a free report

- ❏ Bring your service to life with demonstrations, questions and answers or a speaker slot

- ❏ Show people what results they'll get when they work with you, not how you do it.

GUILDFORD PRINTING.COM, A FRANCHISE

When you run a franchise it's always tempting to use the pre-designed exhibition posters and pull-up stands from head office. The problem with this is that because these are generic, they don't usually take into account your specific aims for the exhibition. Remember how we discussed the importance of matching the expectations of visitors? That means tailored posters and marketing literature. Added to that, when you're marketing any franchised business it's **important that you get the balance right between bespoke design and working within the brand guidelines.** No easy task!

I've always really enjoyed creating our exhibition stands, and over the years have tried to think more and more outside the box. I'd like to share with you what we did at this year's Grow Your Business event. I knew that the recession would be preying on the visitors minds and I wanted to reassure them that the right brand and marketing advice would help them get through the next year.

We led with the strap line **Win More Business with Guildford printing.com: brand and marketing communications specialists.** As usual, we ran a Brand Makeover competition where we gave away a Corporate Identity and Stationery Pack: business cards, letterheads and compliments slips.

"The combination of sponsorship, speaking, and everything I've learned about successful exhibiting resulted in this becoming our most successful exhibition to date."

As well as the brand makeover giveaway, we'd packed 200 goody bags full with paper samples, pens and sweets. We had sherbert boiled sweets (for their colour!) in a bowl on the plinth, along with our piece de resistance: the Grow Your Business seeds. These were a great ice-breaker and also gave us something to talk about after the exhibition. We've even had clients email us images of their plants in full flower: now that's got to be good for building relationships.

As you would probably expect, we thought carefully about every last detail: from the multicoloured sweets we offered passers-by to the traffic light coloured outfits we wore: everything communicated colour and vibrancy!

Having a stand that looks good is all well and good, but the proof is in the pudding as they say. And this year we weren't disappointed. **We left the show with 191 business cards (that's just short of 25% of the total visitors), a dozen or so meetings and some great new relationships forged.**

We're still working through the follow-up so it's too early to give you numbers but progress to date has been very positive.

Having a speaker slot and being a sponsor of the exhibition certainly helped with our exposure and I ensured that we gained maximum value from both. Firstly, as a sponsor our logo was on every piece of online and offline marketing literature. I also submitted plenty of articles to the Grow Your Business blog and made sure I promoted the event at networking events. This didn't directly benefit my business, but it did demonstrate our commitment to helping businesses grow and opened doors with people I may not previously have gained access to.

Later on in the day I made sure either my team or I had spoken to every exhibitor to find out how their day had gone. We often gain valuable business from exhibitors, both before and after the show so this was a worthwhile exercise.

Speaking on branding also tied in very nicely with my objectives for the event and also the competition we were running. We made sure our stand had plenty of examples of lovely logos we've created for clients which gave us the opportunity for discussion with interested visitors.

CHECKLIST FOR FRANCHISEES:

- ☐ Tailor your marketing literature to the show
- ☐ Work within your brand guidelines
- ☐ Add your own touches but make sure your franchisor approves first!

STOP AND TALK, A GROUP OF MICRO-BUSINESSES

Exhibitions can be tough if you run a micro-business. They can take an incredible amount of money and resource to do well, and if you're the only person in the business it can be very difficult to even find enough people to work the stand with you. It's not surprising that many micro-businesses choose to share stands with other businesses. The trouble is, they rarely manage to pull it off.

Shared stands are often overcrowded, messy and confused at best. Graham Whittle of Going for Growth and his band of four chums are the exception to this rule. Graham runs a marketing and sales growth business and was keen to exhibit at a business start-up show. The challenge was that the costs were prohibitive for him to do alone and he couldn't man the stand alone.

The solution? Get together with three other businesses who provide services to help businesses grow more effectively. And so Graham worked with Automated Marketing Systems, Sightpath, and Webbery Associates to create an all round business growth package for small businesses.

The real challenge was to create a cohesive solution for the stand that didn't confuse visitors. The original concept from the Stop and Talk team was that they'd each have one poster which they'd fill with some of their benefits. I suggested they rethink that idea pretty quickly. The four posters would look messy and would fail to make an impact in the space.

If you're going to share a stand then you need to make it look like you've done that for a reason. What you don't want to communicate to potential visitors is that you're sharing a stand because you can't afford one of your own.

Instead we brought Graham's concept of "Stop! And Talk" to life. Bold, eye catching posters and an offer of on-the-spot marketing and sales advice ensured that Graham and his colleagues had a great day. So much so that they've planned to do another two exhibitions this year!

CHECKLIST FOR MICRO-BUSINESSES

☐ Get organised. Think of one common theme that visitors will benefit from, and use that as your focus

☐ Keep your stand cohesive: resist the temptation for bit posters here and there

☐ Agree how you'll manage the enquiries afterwards and who is responsible for what

EXHIBITION PACKING CHECKLIST

Packing for an exhibition is often a frenetic activity. Here is my checklist, I hope it helps!

FOR YOU

- ☐ Toothbrush
- ☐ Make-up
- ☐ Moisturiser
- ☐ Mints
- ☐ Sweets
- ☐ Bottled water
- ☐ Business cards
- ☐ Flat shoes for the afternoon

FOR YOUR STAND

- ☐ Posters
- ☐ Pop-up stand
- ☐ Pull-up posters
- ☐ Furniture
- ☐ Styling props
- ☐ Giveaways
- ☐ Container for competition
- ☐ Poster for competition

YOUR MARKETING LITERATURE

- ☐ Brochures
- ☐ Leaflets
- ☐ Goody bags
- ☐ Product samples

TO SELL/ DEMONSTRATE

- ☐ Product samples
- ☐ Credit card machine
- ☐ Laptop

UNIQUE TO YOU

- ☐
- ☐
- ☐
- ☐

SAMPLE COMMUNICATION PLAN

You'll need to adapt your communication plan depending on your market and your resources, but here's a sample plan you might like to work from.

TIMESCALE	COMMUNICATION
2 months in advance	Email your database to announce what they'll get from visiting you at the exhibition
4 weeks in advance	Mail invitations to your database
4 weeks in advance	Send a press release announcing your competition/ exhibition offer
3 weeks in advance	Email your database inviting them to the exhibition. Outline the benefits to them
1 week in advance	Remind your database you'll be there
Day before the event	Remind your database what they can win if they visit your stand
Day after the show	Email to thank visitors for coming, remind about show offer, and give result of competition
Immediately after show for next couple of weeks	Telephone calls to catch up with leads
Two weeks after show	Remind of show offer. Send link to downloadable 'how to' guide if appropriate
After two weeks	Integrate into your normal marketing activity

USEFUL CONTACTS

AUTORESPONDERS & EMAIL MARKETING

Mail Chimp http://www.mailchimp.com

Get Response www.GetResponse.com

Constant Contact www.ConstantContact.com

aWeber http://www.aweber.com

DESIGN, PRINT, EXHIBITION STANDS

printing.com *www.printing.com* for great value, full colour litho print and exhibition stands.

Nettl *www.nettl.com* The largest network of neighbourhood web studios, selling fabric displays as well as booking systems and print.

The Image Group *www.imagegroupuk.com* Full service exhibition and sign business with nationwide coverage. From simple banners to full design, build and installs.

ACKNOWLEDGEMENTS

I've always dreamed of writing a book, and the fact that I have fulfilled this ambition is down to many, many people who have: listened while I've asked questions, shared experiences, or just given me support and encouragement along the way. In particular I would like to acknowledge the following people.

Tony Rafferty and Peter Gunning. Thank you for the inspiration, the opportunities and the experience that you both gave me.

Paul Webster. The don of exhibition organising. Thank you for sharing so much of your knowledge and expertise with me to allow this young upstart to create a book.

Mum and Dad, thank you for all your support, encouragement and inspiration. And Mum, thank you for dropping everything to proof read an early draft and encourage me that this book might actually have some value.

Caroline Dann. I owe you so much. Thank you for running the studio with such finesse and organisation to enable me to take a step back and write this (and to have a baby before that of course!).

Thank you to Kerry Spiers, Rob Ingle and Chloe Charlton for doing such a sterling job with our clients so that I can relax knowing that they are in safe hands. Thank you to our lovely customers for providing me with so much experience and fun and for, bravely some might say, agreeing to be in this book.

Tom Evans for your calm, gentle guidance and helping me turn a stream of consciousness into something with structure. Maggie MacMillan for your opinionated pernicketyness and attention to detail.

And to Pete, without whom this book would never have been written. Thank you for your support and encouragement. Thank you for rarely complaining about the long nights of tap-tapping next to you while I 'just get this down'. And thank you for providing so much support and hands-on help with the children, and never complaining about the how the house looks. **This is for you.**

ABOUT THE AUTHOR

Fiona Humberstone lives in an beautiful cottage in the Surrey hills with her husband, three children, and a very old cat.

Fiona sold her print franchise and her brand styling company in 2012 and now spends most of her time writing and running creative workshops for small businesses and design professionals.

She also runs a boutique consultancy practice helping companies sell more creative work and is available for speaking engagements. Fiona released her bestselling title How to Style your Brand in 2015 and her latest book, Brand Brilliance launches May 2017

GET IN TOUCH WITH FIONA

www.fionahumberstone.com
instagram.com/thebrand_stylist

EXHIBITION NEW
FABRIC
DISPLAY RANGE

from

**The world has changed. Businesses are increasingly choosing new fabric
exhibition displays. Why?**

They're better.

They're better looking. No more trying to match up text across multiple panels.
Fabric displays can be as wide as five metres and over two metres tall, yet still be a
single continuous graphic. And the colours look eyepopping.

They're better to carry. Inside each display is a lightweight aluminium frame which
collapses down into a small carry bag. No more lugging massive cases around.

They're better to put up. The frame clips together in a few minutes. Just stretch
over the fabric cover and zip it up. Collapse it back down and be on your way
in minutes.

They're better to re-use. Paper stands get easily creased, scuffed and ripped.
Fabric is flexible. If it gets dirty, stick it in a washing machine.

They're better value. Because they're engineered more simply, fabric displays cost
less than equivalent magnetic pop-up displays. Get more from your budget.

Want to see them in action? There are over 100 Nettl neighbourhood studios in
the UK and Ireland. This edition of Exhibit! is a gift to you from Nettl.

*Find your nearest at **www.nettl.com** and talk to us
about how we can help with your next expo.*

Ingenious METHODS to

EXHIBIT

& MAGNIFICENTLY

DISPLAY

your wares for
discerning BUSINESSES *like yours*

DISPLAY STANDS

from **£189**

All our freestanding displays are highly portable. Clip together the frames, then pull over the fabric graphic.

Use at networking meetings, exhibitions or for in-store point-of-sale displays.

When it's over, dismantle in minutes and be on your way again – each comes with a carry case.

HOW FABRIC DISPLAYS WORK

Fabric Displays are made up of two main components — a strong, lightweight, tubular aluminium frame and a printed fabric cover.

The 260gsm 'stretch' fabric cover is printed on both sides as standard. Designed to fit snugly over the frame, it is secured at one edge with a zip fastening. The fabric cover is changeable and additional covers can be ordered separately.

These 'next generation' displays deliver maximum impact and completely eliminate the problem of visible join lines on larger displays.

Fabric Display frames utilise a simple 'click together' mechanism.

Each part is numbered for easy identification and quick assembly.

Stretch the fabric graphic over the frame and zip up.

All Fabric Display frames are supplied with a carry bag for easy transportation and storage.

Each stand clicks together in a few minutes and then simply stretch over the printed fabric graphic.

Nº.1 SELLER

PYTHON
POP UP STAND

Our range includes signage for navigation, literature holders, ipad lecterns, TV displays and tables.

AXE
POP UP STAND

KANGAROO
POP UP STAND

bienvenida!

BOOTH
POP UP STAND

MOJITO
COCKTAIL
TABLE

BACKDROPS

from £379

Ever had to build one of those frames with magnetic bars and panels of graphics? Not fun.

Our backdrop displays pop up in minutes. Each has a continuous graphic, so you don't need to worry about lining up panels – stretch your message across the whole stand.

They're double sided too. And the magic of stretchy fabric is you can flip which side is front each time. One message at one event, flip, different message at the next.

Backdrops available in a variety of sizes and styles. Clip them together with optional fixing kit to make L-shaped or U-shaped displays.

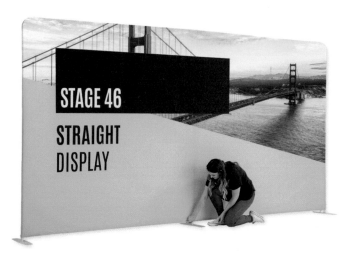

MEETING
BOOTHS

Rent a space-only
stand at your next
expo and pop-up one
of these bad boys –
they're incredible in
real life.

Or use in your office
to make inspirational
booths for solo work
or effective meetings.

Ingenious METHODS to
EXHIBIT
& MAGNIFICENTLY
# DISPLAY
your wares for
discerning BUSINESSES like yours

nettl

Download the full
***Exhibit & Display Guide** at*
www.nettl.com/uk/exhibit

There's a Nettl neighbourhood
web studio near you.

Find your nearest at **www.nettl.com**
and download a copy of our latest
Exhibit & Display Guide,
or ask us for a printed copy.

nettl®

NOW *with OVER*
100 STUDIOS
NATIONWIDE